THE WESLEYAN THEOLOGY SERIES

I0081244

Christian Ethics

Timothy R. Gaines

f▸

THE FOUNDRY
PUBLISHING®

Cover design: Arthur Cherry
Interior design: Sharon Page

Library of Congress Cataloging-in-Publication Data

Names: Gaines, Timothy R., 1981- author.
Title: Christian ethics / Timothy R. Gaines.
Description: Kansas City, MO : The Foundry Publishing, [2021] | Series: The Wesleyan theology series | Includes bibliographical references. | Summary: "One of the primary aims of Christian ethics is to discover how we can convert our work toward God's purposes so that God can make our work holy. In this book, Gaines illuminates this topic as something the people of God can use to reorient our lives toward the way of Jesus and the mission of God in the world. Christians are called to action in God's created world, which is why reasoning engages practice in the chapters of this book so that Wesleyan readers can think and act morally in ways that are faithfully Christian and holy in response to the leading of God"— Provided by publisher.
Identifiers: LCCN 2021021016 (print) | LCCN 2021021017 (ebook) | ISBN 9780834140820 (paperback) | ISBN 9780834140837 (ebook)
Subjects: LCSH: Christian ethics—Nazarene authors. | Church of the Nazarene—Doctrines. | Wesley, John, 1703-1791—Influence. | Christian life—Nazarene authors. | Methodism.
Classification: LCC BJ1251 .G27 2021 (print) | LCC BJ1251 (ebook) | DDC 241—dc23
LC record available at https://lccn.loc.gov/2021021016
LC ebook record available at https://lccn.loc.gov/2021021017

A complete catalog record for this book is available from the Library of Congress.

*Gratefully dedicated in memory of Gordon Gaines,
whom I am humbly proud to call Dad. He guided me in
the pattern of rendering work that was faithful, good,
and holy. Though he heard only the passages I read aloud
to him while the manuscript was a work in progress,
each page of this text is saturated with his influence,
and the reality of its completion is a testimony to
his self-giving kindness and loving support.*

Contents

Acknowledgments

The joy of writing is only expanded when it is considered in light of the many partners along the journey who have made this work possible. I'm grateful for two faculty research grants made available by Trevecca Nazarene University and capably managed by Ruth Kinnersley. Samuel Powell's hospitality through the Wesleyan Center for 21st Century Studies at Point Loma Nazarene University gave me the opportunity to research Wesley's work in a familiar setting on the campus where I first became acquainted with his legacy and where I came to receive it as a gift. Garret Smotherman and Cory Miller provided substantial and capable research support, diligently delivering insightful readings of Wesley's works, and I'm grateful for their partnership. Thanks also to Al Truesdale for his careful reading and insightful analysis of the manuscript; this book is better for his thorough attention.

I'm grateful to several classes of ethics students at Trevecca Nazarene University, both undergraduates and graduate students, and the Covenant Class at Trevecca Community Church, who have listened to developing versions of some of this book. Walking the path of studying ethics with groups like these is a joy and privilege, especially when they're willing to travel with you as partners along the way.

There were more summer mornings than I can count when my parents, Gordon and Marilyn, and my sister,

Renée, welcomed my children into their life and work rhythms so I could write. On most of those mornings, I was taking up a table and receiving the delicious hospitality of Mary Anne and the rest of the team at Moss Rose Bakery in Oakdale, which is still my favorite place to spend a morning putting words on paper.

Thanks also to my wife, Shawna, my son, Callen, and my daughter, Evalynne, for patiently enduring my unnecessarily detailed explanations of exciting discoveries, the encouragement to press on through setbacks, major life changes, and challenges none of us expected to experience or endure. More than that, though, thanks for being icons of new creation hope and for opening to me the continual reminder that "the more excellent way" of love can happen in the things of everyday life.

Introduction
The Way of Wesleyan Ethics

The world isn't waiting for us to get our ethics figured out—and neither are Christians. Every day, a dizzying array of moral challenges presses in. Every day, we make choices between *this* instead of *that*. We face imperfect options because we live in an imperfect world. Moment by moment, we engage in the work of ethics. The only question is whether we realize it. You and I will never avoid ethics.

The question, then, is *how* we'll go about the work of ethics. We need to consider whether we've considered why we do what we do. We need to ask about the kind of character we want to be forming in the midst of our everyday lives. Is there a moral vision that is really guiding us? When we give ourselves a few minutes to really think about it, what truly guides us as we make our decisions from day to day or moment to moment? Even if we can identify *why* we've done something, we then must confront the challenging question of ethics: is what we've done *good*?

I issue, then, this invitation: Are you willing to consider what makes something good? Will you peel back the layers to determine where you are getting your vision of goodness? Within the first week of studying ethics, many of my students come to an interesting realization: they've never really examined what motivates their moral decisions or whether those decisions are consistent. Most of the time they exhibit a desire to be good people, but how they determine what "good" is remains mysterious.

Behind that is a vision of what a good life really looks like. At some level, most of us probably operate with a vision of "the good life" and make decisions in accordance with that vision. Take a moment to identify what vision of the good life is motivating you. Chances are, that vision is actively shaping your ethics.

While there are a number of ways to approach the topic of Christian ethics, my goal in this book is to treat ethics as a call to align ourselves with what God is doing to make creation new. That alignment creates an ethics that takes seriously the fallen state of the world but does not consider fallenness to be our guiding vision for a moral life. In the bold optimism that is characteristic of the Wesleyan tradition, we affirm that God is working in the world to make it new, and our ethics stem from being transformed by and joining that work.

One of the motivating forces in the life and ministry of eighteenth-century reformer John Wesley was that God wasn't waiting to do something about the world's problems. The way Wesley saw it, God was actively working in the world to make all things new, including people whose lives could be joined to God's redemption project. Because the Wesleyan vision sees everyday folks as being made capable of joining that work, the vision of the good life it proclaims is a life fully aligned with the aims and methods God is using to make the world new.

God hasn't made these aims and methods a secret. Christian ethics don't need to uncover a hidden, inscrutable moral code. Very publicly, God became flesh in the person of Jesus. The incarnation of Jesus was God binding Godself to the world in the flesh of a working man. Wide open to the power of God's life-giving Spirit, Jesus's life was a full and vivid example of the good life. His death was a direct engagement of new creation within the old. His resurrection left open the real possibility of *us* living the new creation life too. This, then, is the challenging invitation to Christian ethics: trust that the image of the good life is seen in Jesus of Nazareth, and open yourself to joining his pattern through the power of the Spirit.

We shouldn't let the pious overtones of this approach blunt the sharp edges of the challenge. Jesus's new creation life wasn't situated comfortably in the midst of the old creation. He wasn't simply a kinder, nicer version of old creation. His life and ministry were a *rupture* of the old. It was new creation bursting in, like new wine bursting an old wineskin (Mark 2:22). Jesus's crucifixion stands as a testimony to old creation's way of pushing back against new creation.

Unfinished though the new creation remains, it has decisively begun in Jesus, and his followers are now called to walk in that reality. A new creation ethics takes its moral cues from God's finished project, seen especially in the book of Revelation. "I am making everything new!" John hears from God's throne (Rev. 21:5). The dynamics of this newness guide the moral vision being presented in this book: an uninterrupted union between God and humanity that establishes flourishing human relationships; a decisive dissolution of the people, systems, and structures that seek to dismantle the goodness of creation; and a mutually beneficial relationship between the earth and its inhabitants. The possibility to live in those dynamics stands open to us today. The empty tomb of Jesus is a moral challenge to step into these dynamics, and it is also the means of joining them.

A Wesleyan approach to the moral life accepts this challenge and seeks to engage it head on. In the fervent trust that God is making all things new in Jesus, Wesleyans do not shy away from old creation realities but engage them with the confidence that new creation has already opened in the midst of the old. Our ethics are grounded in the future God is making.

John Wesley's life was marked by his many engagements with old creation's perplexing moral problems. Slavery, poverty, lack of access to heathcare, and diminished educational opportunities were all issues he engaged. A man in perpetual motion, John Wesley was, like many of us, working out his ethics in response to complex moral issues. He was interested in seeing real-life situations change, especially for those who were being harmed. His ministry engaged the world around him, causing scholars to describe him as a "practical theologian."

The work of practical theology, though, was never far from Wesley's focus on God's grace transforming and redeeming human motivation. He described it as "holiness of heart and life." In the language of ethics, the heart has to do with *character*. As the seat and engine of human motivation, the heart is holy when it is entirely God-directed. When this is the case, we are dealing with a human being who has begun participating in God's means of making creation new; a human being whose redeemed motivations guide them to join in the work of new creation. This is why Wesley never seemed interested in developing a general moral theory of generic goodness. Instead he was captivated by the pressing questions "How is the gospel of Jesus working *here*?" and "What is the gospel of Jesus doing *now*?"

If we are going to provide an account of Christian ethics in a Wesleyan way, I suggest we draw from Wesley's own method. I offer an approach to Christian ethics that calls upon followers of Jesus to really engage in the work of ethics in our everyday lives, together responding to the transformative grace that aligns us with God's new creation project. That will require us to take a serious account of just how God is making this world new, and acquire the moral courage to ask how we can be a new creation people in the midst of complex moral situations. Of course, I have no way of knowing what kind of daily situations you may face as you hold this book in your hands, so I offer here a field guide, of sorts, to doing ethics in the real world with an eye toward new creation. It's an approach that will call on us to discern how the news of God making the world new works in *this* situation and calls us to act in *that* way.

You are, of course, welcome to read this book on its own, and you may even find it useful on its own. It may be helpful to know, though, that this book is part of a series on Christian doctrine in the Wesleyan tradition. While I can't replicate what each of the other authors is doing in the other books in the series, many of the chapters in this one will attend to the distinctive features of Christian faith in the Wesleyan tradition. When doctrine is done well, it's more than teaching some ideas for the sake of being right. It is, rather, the way a community goes about trying to say what is most true about God, the world, and ourselves. One approach to Christian doctrine as a Wesleyan is to say, "We confess that the God of Jesus Christ is working to make the world new through the way of Jesus and in the power of the Spirit." The work of ethics, then, is a call to align ourselves with that confession in the midst of everyday decisions and real-world moral dilemmas. My hope is that you might begin to develop a moral imagination for the possible ways in which *any* situation might be engaged. In short, Christian ethics is about developing the kind of *character* that aligns us with God's new creation.

Christian ethics is also the work discerning how we live out the reality of God's redemption. It involves facing down real, on-the-ground situations and stepping into them in the confident hope of Christ's resurrection from the dead and lordship over all creation. It is using the moral decisions we make as an opportunity to bear witness to God's work in the world, up to and including martyrdom. It is speaking into a situation in the conviction that we humans have been created to be in union with a holy and loving God. It is prayerfully asking God to grant the grace that allows our engagement in the world to be converted to the way of Jesus Christ—acting, then reflecting on whether our actions were faithful, then returning to prayer, asking God to correct us where our steps were out of step with the world as Christ is redeeming it.

All of this assumes that doctrine isn't simply what Christians hold in mind as ideas. Christian doctrine is our attempt to tell the truth about the world based on God's activity. For as long as Christian faith has been around, it has been pointing to God's action in the world and saying, "Look! Do you see what's happening here? This is what's really going on!" Christian ethics is the reasoned deliberation on how we might, in Christian community and through the Spirit's enablement, pattern life according to the truth of God's activity in the world. "Christianity is not principally something people think or feel or say," Stanley Hauerwas and Samuel Wells remind us. Instead, they go on, "it is something people do. The narrative of the Gospels is the story of what Christ *did*, and what God did in Christ, and the scriptural narrative shapes and inspires disciples to go and do likewise."[1]

That, to me, seems entirely Wesleyan. Wesley could hardly conceive of a Christian faith that wasn't moving people into the action of God's truth. "Almost Christians" are what Wesley called those who are satisfied with the moral teachings of the great philosophers and who live their lives according to a generalized code of ethics that simply prevents them from stealing or cheating or lying to one another.[2] Christian life, though, was something entirely more.

---

1. Stanley Hauerwas and Samuel Wells, "Why Christian Ethics Was Invented" in *The Blackwell Companion to Christian Ethics*, Stanley Hauerwas and Samuel Wells, eds. (Oxford: Blackwell Publishing, 2006), 37.

2. John Wesley, "The Almost Christian" in *The Works of John Wesley*, Thomas Jackson, 3rd ed. (Grand Rapids: Baker Books, 2005), 1:17.

There was, for him, a "more excellent way" that was nothing other than the fullness and delight of a life fully aligned to God's new creation, filled with love for God and neighbor.[3]

"The more excellent way" is a phrase borrowed primarily from Paul (1 Cor. 12:31) that is also the title of one of John Wesley's sermons. Neither turns this phrase into permission to live in a sense of moral superiority over others but, rather, use it to signal a way of living more fully into God's new creation work. For Paul, who coined the term, and Wesley, who elaborated on it, the "more excellent way" is holy love. "If I give all I possess to the poor and give over my body to hardship that I may boast, but do not have love, I gain nothing," Paul writes (1 Cor. 13:3).

John Wesley expanded this theme when he wrote a sermon titled after Paul's phrase, making a distinction between a "lower path" and a "higher path."[4] The lower path, as he describes it, is not morally wrong. It includes "doing many good works, abstaining from gross evils, and attending the ordinances of God." The more excellent way, though, is a life that is completely *transformed* by holy love. It is to be motivated to move beyond the basic vision of being a vaguely good person and "to aspire to the heights and depths of holiness—after the entire image of God."[5]

Summed up, the message of the Wesleyan tradition is that God is redeeming the world in a way that allows us to do more than muddle through life doing the bare moral minimum. There is a more excellent way, a vision of the good life that includes all of our motivations shot through with self-giving love in the way of Jesus Christ. More than being a nebulously good person who simply avoids doing

---

3. Wesley, "The Almost Christian," 1:24.

4. Wesley, "Sermon 89: The More Excellent Way," http://wesley.nnu.edu/john -wesley/the-sermons-of-john-wesley-1872-edition/sermon-89-the-more -excellent-way/.

5. Wesley, "The More Excellent Way."

bad things, the more excellent way enlivens us for joyful and free moral participation in God's redemption project. Filled with hope, the Wesleyan tradition affirms that the world isn't waiting for God to finally get around to doing something about the brokenness and sorrow that we encounter on a daily basis. Instead, it points to what God is doing to bring renewal to a creation that groans for redemption.

Wesley didn't condemn those who walk the lower path, and neither should we. In his view, they do so by God's grace and as God's children. But Wesley was never satisfied with being only vaguely associated with the transforming love of God. Throughout his life, his singular pursuit was God's love. It was a well without a bottom, a cathedral without a ceiling, a reservoir without a limit. Why not, then, plunge headlong into the depths of love? Wesley's more excellent way is the life of those who gratefully receive and insatiably pursue divine love that knows no bounds, allowing that love to shape the way they live and work in the world.

That's why I'm hoping you'll use this book in the company of fellow disciples. Perhaps you are looking for guidance in the midst of a challenging situation, or perhaps you hope to engage everyday life with clearer moral vision. Either way, the chapters of this book are meant to draw us into the dynamic vision of the way Wesleyans see God working in the world. They are meant to fuel a conversation among a group of Jesus followers who ask, "What does it look like for God's new creation work to happen *here*, among *our* lives? How is creation being made new *here*? How can we join in?"

Part 2 comprises discernment dialogues, which are designed to engage more specifically some contemporary moral issues. The dialogues are designed to pose questions and open approaches as you discern a moral pathway in light of God's new creation. I'm not sitting with you in the unique complexities of your own situation, so these aren't designed to be quick answers or detailed blueprints. I offer them as a pathway of discernment. I hope they offer a helpful approach to the conversation and that they will open some moral possibilities to you as you consider them in light of what God is doing to make the world new.

Beginning the Work of Christian Ethics

Part I

The Work of Christian Ethics

The morning was still new when a young man approached the shore of the lake and found there a group of workers concluding their day's labors. Their bearded faces were sun-baked and deeply lined. Their arms, backs, and legs carried the evidence of the hardscrabble work that had shaped their bodies since they were young. Rough, calloused hands skillfully manipulated their equipment while the men joked with one another in the unrefined dialect of those whose circumstances had pressed them into a trade, rather than the opportunities a formal education could have afforded them. Maybe it wouldn't matter anyway, since they lived so far from the center of political power and philosophical discovery. These were men of lake and land who strained every day to extract a living from the unforgiving earth. There, on the shoreline of a lake in northern Israel, where the water-work of fishermen met the soil-work of farmers, Jesus struck up a conversation.

He talked to them about fishing and even gave them some advice on their lifelong craft. When his suggestion resulted in a boat full of fish, they were ready to listen to what else he had to say. But Jesus didn't say much. He didn't use the opportunity to astound them with the depth of his insight or dazzle them with his intellect. Rather, he called them to follow him—to walk away from the family business, to step away from the only lives they had ever known, and to take the journey of a lifetime (Luke 5:1–11).

If we are looking for somewhere to start exploring Christian ethics, the shore of that lake would be a good choice. What happened there was a call to some everyday people to catch a glimpse of God's work in the midst of a fallen world and to tune their lives to that work. There, God became bound up with the work of a groaning creation, an intermingling that altogether affirmed the Creator's commitment to everyday people—and in particular with those whose everyday lives are hard.

Whatever we might eventually say about Christian ethics, we must remember the people on the shore of the Galilean sea, working to scratch out a simple life for themselves. Among those people Jesus issued his first call to follow him and his ways. Jesus's call was not a clever doctrinal theory or thought experiment. It came to real people in the midst of their real lives, and called them to real action in the midst of real situations: "Follow me."

In this sense, Jesus did not offer them "ethics," if by that word we mean a set of organized principles by which lives are ordered. Jesus's teachings were not moralistic life lessons that one could easily consume and go on their way. No, his teachings made claims upon their lives and called on them to follow his way. His teachings do not float above the lives of his followers but are deeply connected to the realities of their everyday lives, what they do, how they arrange their lives, and whom they follow.

The realities of everyday life are what I'll call "work." Not to be confused with our jobs, work in this context is the way our flesh interacts with the world around us. It is what we do with our bodies—the actions we give to this embodied life. Each and every day, we align our work toward particular ends or goals. We reach for an apple with the aim of gaining nutrition, for example. We press the flesh of our

Holy work is not holy because it pristinely hovers above the mundane and ordinary tasks of human life. It is holy because it gathers those tasks up and works them according to the new creation that is opening up to us in Jesus.

fingertips onto computer keyboards, we plop our tired bones down in the front seat of a car and drive home after a long shift, we open our arms and embrace a loved one, holding their flesh close to ours. This is our work.

Our work is something we may be paid to do, though that is not always the case. For about eight hours of most days, full-time employees give their bodies to the work of their jobs. The movements they make and the ways they use their bodies are aimed at repairing appliances, teaching children, harvesting fruit, designing graphics, or painting houses. When the shift is over, though, work does not stop. There is the work of making dinner, tending to finances, playing with children, and the work of resting. Work is what we *do*.

Christian ethics, then, are *worked* ethics. This is not to say that they are not also thoughtful but that they are not exclusively intellectual—because such a thing would be too far separated from the work of our flesh. In the same way that Israelite fishermen did not have the luxury of catching theoretical fish, Christian ethics does not have the luxury of being reduced to theoretical enterprise. Instead, Jesus calls those who are in the middle of their work.

The Sanctification of Our Work

His call is not to stop work, though. Rather, he calls us to redirect our work toward his purposes. "I see that you are doing some work," Jesus might have said to the sons of Zebedee. "Now, what if I taught you to direct that work toward the new creation I am bringing? Let's talk about how one fishes according to my purposes." The journey that began on that lakeshore was a master class in learning to reflect on one's work and to aim that work toward holiness. Holy work is not holy because it pristinely hovers above the mundane and ordinary tasks of human life. It is holy because it gathers those tasks up and works them according to the new creation that is opening up to us in Jesus.

We could say that the work of those Galilean fishermen underwent a *conversion*. It was turned toward God's purposes. It was made holy. Fishing for food became fishing for people. The direction of their work took a distinctly different turn, but their calluses did not disappear. They were still fishermen, even as their nets became a distant memory.

One of the primary questions of Christian ethics is how our work can be converted to God's purposes—or made holy. Our work is converted—*sanctified*—rather than abandoned or erased. In directing it toward God's purposes, our work is not obliterated, but it is given up as an act of praise to the one who has lovingly spoken creation into good order. The work of our lives, sanctified toward holy aims, is nothing more than the faithful response we give to the Word that has been spoken to us. Sanctified work is our "amen" offered in response to what God has spoken first.

A Christian ethics in the Wesleyan tradition opens the possibility that we don't need to leave our work, our training, or even ourselves. It does inquire as to whether those things are aligned toward the new creation God is bringing. It helps us find where our work may not be entirely attuned to new creation and calls upon us to make adjustments. In calling those fishermen to follow, Jesus didn't tell them to stop being Galilean fishermen. He didn't tell them their lack of formal education had to be remedied or that they were going to need to start acting a bit more like Jerusalem sophisticates rather than the backwater fishermen they were. The call to discipleship as it came to the sons of Zebedee did not ignore the real situations of their lives. They were still fishermen. They continued to speak with Galilean accents (Matt. 26:73). They were still workers.

Our own work may be the work of healing, parenting, teaching, caring for children or the elderly, communicating, delivering, reading, repairing, growing, or selling—and all of these are capable of undergoing a conversion to be performed as acts of discipleship. The question Christian ethics asks is about where that work is going. It is the option Jesus placed in front of a group of water workers. They had once pressed their flesh into the work of catching fish, but from this point on, their work would be fishing for people. These were men who were not converted from workers to non-workers. (How could this be possible? Our work persists as long as we are flesh.) Rather, their work was *converted* toward a different aim—it was sanctified. Christian ethics cannot only be a set of moral ideals or ethical principles. It must ask about real-life realities and reflect vigorously on how our work in those realities can be converted to the way of Jesus. It asks how our work aims toward new creation in the midst of an old, fallen, and groaning creation. It is the ongoing task of working, reflecting, adjusting, and working again—all while the call of Jesus rings in our ears: *Follow me, and I will teach you a new way to work.*

The Renewed Heart in the Work of Christian Ethics

So long as we are learning how to align our work with the new–life reality Jesus opens to us, we need to reflect on that work and ask whether it happened according to the prayer Jesus taught us: "on earth as it is in heaven." Christian ethics cannot consist of working without reflecting on whether what we've done has been fully committed to the kingdom that Jesus initiated. Yet neither can it consist of reflecting without working. Reason alone will not convert our work to the way of Jesus. Even if we perfectly conceived of such work, there's no guarantee we would actually do it. This is why the work of Christian ethics will also need to involve the seat of our motivation—or what the biblical writers refer to as the heart.[1]

One of the distinctive affirmations of the Wesleyan tradition is the belief in *orthokardia*—the idea that we must be people of right *hearts* alongside our right practices and right beliefs.[2] In the shadow of the Reformation and the Enlightenment, some approaches to ethics highlight how one comes to have the right ideas that are convincing enough to shape someone's actions. The Wesleyan tradition does not dismiss rigorous intellectual reflection but recognizes its limits. It asks serious questions about whether the Christian moral life is about finding the right *ideas* about God and then structuring a set of ethics to fit that information.

Even if we were able to get all of our ideas in order and somehow gain an utterly complete idea of God, there is nothing to say that those ideas alone would move us to action. We could tick every ethical box with a sense of drudgery, anger, or fear. Even those who are convinced of the perfection of their ideas can be miserable people whose ethical motivation revolves around willing themselves through the moral hoops of life. That isn't the vision of the moral life in the Wesleyan tradition, though. For Wesley, holiness is happiness, and the moral life is the gift of delight.

Humans are creatures whose hearts link the intellect to our motivations; thought and action are united in and directed by the heart. The heart uniting the intellect with action is what John Wesley understood to be a heart that was rightly related to God. In that relationship, the human

---

1. Drawing from the biblical writers, the Wesleyan tradition imagines the human being as one whose life is unified at the heart. The heart is the center of our *motivation*.

2. The Greek word *kardia* translates into English most often as "heart," and it is where we derive terms like "cardiology," the medical study of the heart. See Gregory S. Clapper, *John Wesley on Religious Affections: His Views on Experience and Emotion and Their Role in the Christian Life and Theology* (Metuchen, NJ: Scarecrow Press, 1989).

becomes an *orthokardia* being, with a heart aligned toward new creation. Envisioning ethics this way is as much a matter of the heart as it is the brain. While ethics is about the decisions we make, it's also about the *way* those decisions are made at a precognitive level—the way our heart motivates us.

At this point the Wesleyan tradition's grand promise speaks: our hearts can be transformed by God's love! An enduring Wesleyan proclamation, says Theodore Runyon, "is Wesley's insistence that the renewal of the image of God involves the creature in actual transformation—no less than re-creation."[3] Although reason is involved, this approach isn't about merely *thinking* our way into new creation action but about allowing the love of God to so fill our hearts that all of our work becomes converted to the way of Jesus.

Why Christian Ethics Doesn't Apply to Your Life

This is why Christian ethics does not *apply* to our lives. My work includes teaching ethics to college students at a Christian university. The young and energetic people who fill the classroom semester after semester are usually compelled to be there because of a course requirement. The problem some of them express at the beginning of the course is, "I'm not sure how this class is going to apply to my major." They are aspiring musicians, teachers, business professionals, and engineers, so why should they have to take a course that isn't going to provide them some kind of skill that can directly benefit their chosen profession?

Many are surprised when I agree with them. "You're right," I tell them. "This class does not *apply* to your major.

---

3. Theodore Runyon, *Exploring the Range of Theology* (Eugene, OR: Wipf and Stock, 2012), 175.

This class is meant to make sense of your major." What I don't make explicit in those first days of class is that I hope their imagination for ethics will be far more than simply layering ethical principles on top of whatever it is they are already doing. I want their work to be turned to God's purposes—sanctified. More than wanting them to be nicer, kinder, more ethical, or well-adjusted students of their vocations, I want—in the same way Jesus wanted for the sons of Zebedee—them to give their work to a way that produces something more than fish. I want them to come to an understanding of ethics in a distinctively Christian sense that converts their work to the new creation God is bringing in Jesus Christ.

A similar dynamic emerges in my work as a preacher. The pressure to make sure the sermons "apply" to the lives of the people is hard to ignore. Often, that can take the form of a preacher offering tips and tricks for those under their pastoral care to become a bit more emotionally well adjusted to do their work for the week. The word-working that a Christian preacher does, however, is to open a story in which worshipers can find themselves and, in so doing, have their own work converted to the rhythms of that story.

The steelworker who gathers in worship can find that his work's meaning is not measured by his employer's stock price but by the way his work can be made holy as it is converted to the work God is doing to redeem this world. If the high school student in the congregation comes to a sermon from Luke's Gospel expecting it to help her find answers to her physics homework, she will almost certainly be disappointed that the sermon did not "apply to her life." If the preacher has done their word work well, though, the physics student can discover that her own work of study can be converted toward Christ's purposes. She now learns physics for the sake of the new creation, and the gospel is what makes sense of her physics homework.

The idea that Christian ethics should be applied to our lives assumes that ethics can somehow be layered on top of a life without radically reorienting that same life. Christian ethics, though, will only make sense in light of conversion. This is why I don't think Peter or James and John would have cared for a discussion about ethics. Whatever ethics were for these fishers-turned-disciples, they were wrapped up in Jesus's call to give themselves to the way of discipleship and orient their work toward Christ's new creation purposes.

Jesus was not providing tips and tricks on how to be a more ethical version of a fisherman through the application of a few moral principles. Jesus issued a call to discipleship, and the pattern of life that emerged as Peter, James, and John turned and walked away from the boats is what Christian ethics is after. Christian ethics wants to know how a fisherman's work can be converted to fish for people, how a nurse's work can be sanctified toward the kind of healing Jesus demonstrated, or how a salesperson's work can be turned toward the kind of thing Jesus was doing in feeding the multitudes. Sometimes it calls us to leave the boats when our work is simply incompatible with the way of life Jesus offers. Christian ethics wants to know how the work of churches can be made holy as a foretaste of creation being made new. All of this assumes that Christian ethics cannot be a set of principles that are simply *applied* to the way we are already working.

If any set of ethics makes a claim to be Christian, they must be lived, walked, and embodied. They are the kind forged in the space between the soil turned by struggling farmers and the water worked by fishermen whose livelihood depended on that day's catch, and then turned toward new creation. They are the kind that isn't satisfied with making a nicer version of a worker but is interested in the more excellent way of all of that person's work being converted by love toward God's new creation project. They will live in the down-to-earth lives of those who work and toil and who encounter Jesus in the midst of their efforts. Christian ethics does its work with calluses on its hands— not only because it came first as a calling to workers but also because it is the work that those who follow Jesus are called to do.

The Tools of the Trade

If Christian ethics is *worked* ethics, we need to take account of the tools we use to do this work and how that work is done. The vision guiding us and the kind of tools we use to do the work will shape the kind of work we do. Throughout my childhood and adolescence, I developed an interest in woodworking at my father's side, watching him carefully transform planks of lumber into desks, tables, cabinets, beds, and other interesting and beautiful keepsakes. Eventually, I undertook a few projects of my own. Sitting down in front of his library of woodworking magazines, I searched their pages for a project that matched my technical skill but also met the requirements of the tools we had. Even my rudimentary understanding of woodworking told me that the plans in front of me were going to guide the work I would undertake and that my ability to use certain tools to accomplish that plan would be essential.

Before beginning the work of ethics, we need a vision that guides the work. Like a carpenter beginning a project, we need plans drawn up so we know what we are working toward. That vision is what ethicists refer to as a vision of *goodness*, or "the good life." If ethics is determining what kind of work ought to be done to work toward goodness, we also need to know exactly what vision of goodness we are working toward. Wise carpenters draw up plans before starting a project, and the same should be true for the work of ethics.

The trouble is that we rarely take the time to form a moral vision of goodness before we begin ethical work. We take up the work and make choices, but those choices are sometimes inconsistent or haphazard. "It depends on the situation," we often say. While situations are undoubtedly different, do we work from a consistent vision of goodness in diverse situations, or does the situation itself overpower our vision of goodness? The ancient Greek philosopher Socrates saw his task as one of helping people out of this trap. In his estimation, "the unexamined life is not worth living."[1] Socrates continually encountered unexamined lives marked by inconsistent application of moral principles.

"It's good to prosecute a murderer," his friend Euthyphro said to Socrates—unless that murderer happened to be his own father and the victim was of lower social standing.[2] Among such directionless reasoning, Socrates saw his role as prompting people to be more specific when they said that something was "good." What made it good?

Because we are often imprecise about what we mean when we say something is good, we struggle to work from a clear vision of goodness and, therefore, struggle to know how to employ the tools of ethics. We may operate with a vague sense of what is good and bad, but when pressed, we find it difficult to name what exactly makes something good or bad.

Is something good because it produces a favorable result for me?

Is it good because it benefits many people, even if I don't know them?

Are there some things that are simply good no matter what consequence they produce?

---

1. Plato, *Apology*, in *Five Dialogues: Euthyphro, Apology, Crito, Meno, Phaedo*, trans. G. M. A. Grube, rev. John M. Cooper, 2nd ed. (Indianapolis: Hackett Publishing Company, Inc., 2002), 41.

2. Plato, *Euthyphro*, in *Five Dialogues*, 1–20.

In these few questions, we see how difficult it can be to pin down "goodness." Without a clear vision of goodness, though, how can we do the work of ethics?

The tools we'll examine now aren't necessarily exclusive to *Christian* ethics, but many Christians have used them. What remains distinctive about Christian ethics is its *vision* of goodness that guides the use of these tools. The vision of goodness I propose is seen in Jesus of Nazareth and his distinct way of making the world new. If a tool can help us shape life toward that reality, we may have the vision of goodness that we need to know how to use the tools.

Taking Account of the Tools

The most common tools in the workshop of ethics in the Western tradition are the duty tool, the results tool, the God tool, and the virtue tool.[3] As I provide a brief description of each, take a moment to consider how each one works and what kind of ethics it would produce if we were to put it into action.

The Duty Tool

Most basically, a duty-based approach to ethics, called "deontology" (from the Greek term *deon*, meaning "duty" or "ought"), says that some acts are simply right and others are wrong, regardless of the consequences they produce. A classic example is lying. Taking a duty-based approach to lying would say that lying is wrong no matter what and that a person should not lie because doing so gives permission to all persons to lie in all cases. Immanuel Kant (1724–1804), who is the champion of duty-based approaches to

---

3. For a more detailed introductory account of these theories and how they shape ethics, I recommend Robin W. Lovin, *Christian Ethics: An Essential Guide* (Nashville: Abingdon Press, 2000); and Craig A. Boyd & Don Thorsen, *Christian Ethics and Moral Philosophy: An Introduction to Issues and Approaches* (Grand Rapids: Baker Academic, 2018).

ethics, refers to this as the principle of universality. We can determine that an act is good if we can elevate it universally so that it is good for all people in all times and all places. When we use this tool, stealing can always be wrong because, if we consider it morally good to let one person in one circumstance steal, then we also need to allow that it is morally good for all people to steal no matter the circumstance. Kant would not have viewed Robin Hood with much sympathy.

Those who reach for the duty tool are often attracted to its relative simplicity in the way it quickly eliminates ambiguity from moral situations. The ethical project that results is one that often boasts clean edges and clear lines between right and wrong. The duty tool doesn't have to deal with measuring whether the consequences of using it are good; it simply slices between good and bad acts, consequences be what they may.

In a duty-based approach to ethics, one measures goodness in the act itself.

There are, of course, those who find the duty-based tool to be too blunt. Their critiques often point to the relative lack of attention a duty-based approach gives to the consequences of an act.

Let's suppose, for a moment, that you receive a news alert that a dangerous serial killer is on the loose in your neighborhood. Minutes later, there is a knock at the door. Peering through the window, you see a disheveled man standing on your doorstep who matches the description of the serial killer.

He makes eye contact and asks, "Is your son home right now?"

Let's also say that you know your son *is* home, watching TV in the next room. At this point, you have a choice: should you lie to the man or tell him the truth? At its most basic, the duty-based approach maintains that lying is always wrong—therefore, lying to this man would be wrong.

Regardless of the consequences, you tell the man, "Yes, he's here."

Reaching for the duty-based tool has created an ethical reality in that moment.

The Results Tool

Another approach to ethics measures goodness according to the consequences a given act produces (called "consequentialism"). Reaching for this tool means you are prepared to create a moral reality in which the results matter most. John Stuart Mill (1806–1873), who was a primary proponent of this approach, was fond of saying that the results of an act can be measured according to the amount of happiness it produces. If an act results in more people being happy than those who are unhappy, it should be considered a morally superior act to one that produces less happiness for fewer people. Mill's approach has also been called "utilitarianism," or what results in the greatest amount of good for the biggest number of people. In this case, Robin Hood would be a moral champion. Yes, one or two rich people might be unhappy with Robin's thievery, but ten or twelve poor people might be able to feed their children, so that makes it a good act.

Those who prefer to build with this tool often point to the product that it produces. Though it is not quite as simple as a duty-based approach (Mill makes many distinctions between "higher" and "lower" happiness, for instance), it is well equipped to create moral realities that are measured by the principle of the greatest good for the greatest number of people. Because more people are receiving the benefit, this approach says, this way of working ethics can yield a world in which goodness is found in the maximum number of people bearing the benefit.

In a results-based approach to ethics, goodness is found in whether the act produces beneficial consequences for a majority.

Not everyone is pleased with the kind of project this tool produces, however. Its detractors point to the complications involved with using consequences to determine the goodness of an act. How many times, for example, have you done something that produced an immediately beneficial result, only to learn later that those benefits opened a Pandora's Box of unintended consequences?

Consider a 2003 study that examined the Federal Aviation Administration's policy that young children flying on commercial aircraft in the United States needed to use a safety seat. According to the FAA, the goodness of this policy was in the result it produced: more children would be safe while flying. If an unexpected patch of turbulence, for example, were to arise, a child in a safety seat would be less likely to fall or be injured.

When the policy went into effect, the airlines quickly realized that a young child who would previously have been riding on a parent's lap would now need their own (ticketed) seat. Equally quickly, the airlines jumped at the opportunity to get money for those seats. Now an infant who previously flew for free required a full-fare ticket, and many young families began to opt out of flying, choosing to drive instead. Because road travel is statistically more dangerous than air travel, the results were ultimately tragic: more children died in car accidents who may have survived had they been in the air instead of on the road.[4]

Of course, no one wanted this outcome, but it raises the question of how far down the line of consequences

---

4. Thomas Newman, Brian D. Johnson, and David C. Grossman, "Effects and Costs of Requiring Child-Restraint Systems for Young Children Traveling on Commercial Airplanes," *JAMA Pediatrics* 157, no. 10 (2003): 949–1036.

one must go to determine whether the original act can be judged as good or bad.

The God Tool

Often referred to as "divine command theory," this tool shapes the moral life after the command of God. Because this tends to be a popular approach to Christian ethics in particular, we'll spend a few extra paragraphs exploring its contours. Those who prefer this tool seek to establish the goodness of an act not in the act itself or in the consequence of the act but in whether the act has been commanded by God. Different variations of this tool have been developed, but generally it is favored by those who use it because it provides a foundation outside ourselves as the basis for morality, free from the whims of those who use the tool. Its objectivity is often what motivates moral artisans to reach for it. By using God—who, arguably, has different concerns from us—as the measure of morality, we are better positioned to avoid simply acting and then justifying our actions. The divine command theory is an equal-opportunity critic of all of our motivations and actions; all of our actions are held in the gaze of a morally perfect God.

The divine command theory doesn't come without its challenges, however. Primary among these is the challenge of the ephemeral connection between God's command and our interpretation of God's command. Though the notion of following God's command may appear to be one of the more clear-cut methods, *knowing* what God is command-ing can become tricky. Consider the situation in which someone believes God has told him to do something that seems inconsistent with what God has commanded another person to do. Soldiers fighting on both sides of the United States Civil War, for example, kept up the fight on the prem-ise that they were each on God's side of the battle.

"But what about the Bible?" you may ask. "Hasn't God given us clear commands in Scripture?"

The pages of Scripture are certainly replete with commands, but the way we encounter them is both promising and complex. We will have to wait for a more complete engagement of Scripture's place in the tool chest of Christian ethics, but for now, we will simply identify the challenge of using Scripture in the divine command theory of ethics.

Those who study the Bible soon learn it is a complex set of texts. If one views Scripture as an ethics textbook where clear commands are given, it won't take long to come across a number of apparent moral contradictions. For example, in one book it seems that God allows or even commands violence, while in another book Jesus (who is also God) commands his followers to pray for our enemies rather than kill them. God's rather detailed commands to ancient Israel regarding their diet and dress are another example. Should the prohibitions against consuming pork and shellfish still be in effect for modern Christians (see Lev. 11:7–12)? If we are to take the Bible as a whole, many of its direct moral commands can appear contradictory, inapplicable, or socially inappropriate.

Compounding these complications, the Bible is silent on a host of contemporary issues that press on our moral consciousness today. It has little to say directly about the ethics of human gene splicing, or global trade policy, or the ethics that should guide end-of-life decisions. This is not to suggest that the Bible has no role to play in contemporary Christian ethics (see chapter 3). It is to point out, rather, that Scripture can pose a challenge to the divine command theory.

Additionally, the problem of our own sin and limitations weighs heavily on the divine command theory. When it comes to matters of interpreting God's intentions, a healthy dose of humility can help us realize we are often prone to taking the pieces of the divine command that are most beneficial to ourselves and leaving the rest for some-one else. "But the Bible says," we might say, looking only to the pieces of it that bolster a moral position that may be personally advantageous but remains harmful to others. Numerous scholars have pointed out that institutional slavery was often justified by Christians in the antebellum United States by appealing to the Bible. Even, and perhaps especially, when we are not aware of it, our biases and limited experiences may lead us to adopt an incomplete or flawed view of God's ethical intentions for creation.

The Virtue Tool

Another classical approach to the work of ethics calls upon virtue to be the primary shaper of moral life. Fa-mously, Aristotle placed this tool in the hands of his son, instructing him to learn how to live the good life by finding a person who was already accomplished in living the good life and apprenticing himself to that person.[5] Eventually, the skills he would gain by copying the behavior of the old-er person would allow him to live a flourishing, happy life. When one's life is in proper alignment, Aristotle taught, the capacity to live the good life should become second nature. This requires learning how to keep our impulses aimed down the middle of the moral road. For Aristotle, virtue isn't simply a morally good disposition or act; it is the abili-ty to steer and strike an equal balance between the excesses and deficiencies of our impulses.

Desire for material possession, for example, is an impulse most people share, and Aristotle doesn't find any-thing particularly good or bad about wanting things. What we do with that desire, however, is a different matter entire-ly. If we steer toward excess, we end up gorging ourselves

---

5. Aristotle, *Aristotle's Nicomachean Ethics*, trans. Robert C. Bartlett & Susan D. Collins (Chicago: University of Chicago Press, 2012).

needlessly, satisfying our desire in excessive and unhealthy ways. A deficient approach would mean we choose not to satisfy this desire at all, depriving ourselves and possibly leading to "dishealth." Aristotle locates virtue in the middle way between excess and deficiency.

We may think of desires for academic or spiritual achievement, physical fitness, sex, and the list could go on. Every desire has the potential for excess or deficiency. Perhaps you know the fitness fanatic who spends so much time at the gym that she forgets her family, or the academic animal who is so driven to learn that he neglects his friendships. Alternatively, the person who never exercises or rarely bothers to challenge himself to learn anything new are those who have a deficient approach, according to Aristotle.

Even if you are not persuaded by Aristotle's middle-way approach to virtue, you may find his method interesting. Moral virtue, he said, is acquired through the formation of habits. If you want to become a virtuous person, he said, you practice your way into it. It's not so much that we one day suddenly become convinced of a morally good life as much as we form it in our lives on a regular basis. Consider a professional athlete or instrumentalist. Each becomes good at what they do because they devoted hours to practicing their craft. The same thing goes for the good life, Aristotle says. Practicing a virtuous attitude around having possessions—to return to our original example—will eventually lead to it becoming second nature, and before we know it, we are living virtuously when it comes to the desire for material goods and generosity.

Recently, some moral philosophers have found virtue ethics to be helpful in speaking to the way modern people can approach the good life in the face of so much diversity. As the world becomes smaller through the ever-quickening pace of the exchange of ideas and the proliferation of travel, difference is no longer sequestered an ocean away but is often found in the demographic makeup of our neighbor-hoods or in our children's schools. How can we say any-thing meaningful about morality when so many different people are all sharing space like this? Each community, some have said, maintains its own virtues.[6] Depending on the community, different virtues will be differently regard-ed, and the morally good act is the one that aligns with the accepted virtues of a given community.

To use a silly example, the act of sticking a knife in another person's stomach may not be a virtuous act if you are at an amusement park. If you move into a surgical bay, however, the act of slicing into the abdomen of another human being will likely be seen as virtuous, and the per-son doing it would not only avoid jail but also be highly compensated! The moral goodness of an act is measured according to the way that act aligns with the highest ideals of whatever community in which one finds oneself.

Critics are quick to point out that, when taken to its extreme, this community-based approach to virtue ethics could potentially become insulated, isolated, and harm-ful. We could talk about "virtuous racists," for example, if a community was committed to the principles of racism. Additionally, some opt to leave the virtue tool on the shelf because it doesn't leave clearly marked lines in the final product the way the duty tool does. Sometimes it's difficult to pick out the difference between good and bad in the moral life that is shaped by the virtue tool—mainly because it can be difficult to know when one is departing from the middle way and steering toward one of the ditches of excess or deficiency. Using the virtue tool, though, shapes

---

6. A key representative work in this approach is Alasdair MacIntyre's *Whose Justice? Which Rationality?* (Notre Dame, IN: University of Notre Dame Press, 1988).

the moral life in a way where goodness is found in the act's adherence to a vision of the good life in one's community.

Working with the Tools of Christian Ethics

As much as the metaphor of woodworking tools is helpful to understand how ethics has been approached and why it seems like there are so many ethical projects being developed, it also presents us with the temptation to turn ethics into a way to solve moral problems as quickly and easily as possible simply because we have an array of tools to choose from. The work of ethics involves far more than simply finding the right tool to solve the problem in front of us. In the years that I've taught ethics, I've found that those who are just beginning tend to want to take on the world's moral issues by pulling one of their new tools off the shelf and going to work as efficiently as possible.

"If this is the moral problem we are facing," one of them might say, "I know a moral theory that will solve it quite nicely!"

I hesitate to condone this approach because the work of Christian ethics isn't about simply arriving efficiently at tidy solutions to life's moral problems. Rather, the work of Christian ethics is to learn to do our work in ways that are faithful to the vision of goodness we see in a carpenter from Nazareth and the way he was making the world new.

Returning to the memories of my father's workshop, I can recall my eager impulse to get a project done quickly. Most of the time I could see a pathway that would allow us to get the job done efficiently, even though I knew the finished product wouldn't bear the marks of true crafts-manship. Applying the wisdom that comes from being a far more accomplished carpenter, my dad often proposed an alternative course of action that would be much slower and require more work to set up.

"Why don't we just . . ." I would say, suggesting some expedient solution to the task in front of us.

"Well," he would say, "you *could* do that—but this other way would probably be better."

Every time my dad said something like that, he was channeling an important principle for ethics: there are many ways to address problems, but responsible ethics isn't about quick solutions. Historically, the work of ethics has been concerned with how one carves out work in the world that corresponds with what is *good*—no matter how cumbersome, slow, or costly it may be. While the modern world has shaped us to think that something is good precisely because it is quick, cheap, or easy, the work of ethics calls for a fair amount of suspicion when it comes to equating an *easy* solution with a *good* one. In a world where quick, cheap, and easy have become synonyms for "good," the work of Christian ethics can appear needlessly cumbersome and ill equipped to deliver quick solutions to life's moral problems.

The more excellent way may not be as expedient or as easy. The way Jesus calls his followers to walk is rarely expedient, hardly easy, and never cheap. It is, however, *good*. The work of Christian ethics calls us to learn to work in the way of the new creation that God is bringing about in Jesus. Because that way is not cheap, quick, or easy, it will take a specialized set of tools that are capable of calling a people to the work of new creation and equipping them with the character and skill to do the work.

"We cannot create the new creation," Néstor Míguez helpfully reminds us. "It comes from God as a new earth and a new heaven, which is beyond any human possibility to achieve." At the same time, "New creation is also an invitation to the hope that becomes an impelling force to join in God's labor of giving birth to the new creation, a labor conceived, for our side, as a creative participation in the life of God that manifests the liberty of God's children."[7] Such a vision is going to require making use of the tools that allow us to do the work well.

Christian ethics requires us to engage in the deliberative task of discerning how the work of our lives can be best aligned with the vision of the new creation we see taking place in Jesus. Generally, the name we have given this kind of work is "discipleship." It is the skilled work of walking the particular, peculiar way of Jesus.

What, then, are the tools that allow us to do the unique work of Christian ethics? Though this brief list is by no means exhaustive, these tools can include, among other things:

Prayer

Especially when we pray the way Jesus taught his disciples (see Matt. 6, Luke 11), prayer is more than listing requests. It is also a means of grace that aligns our desires with the new creation God is bringing. "Your kingdom come, your will be done, on earth as it is in heaven" is the kind of request that aligns our desires with God's work.[8]

Scripture

People get confused when we talk about Scripture as a *practice* because we usually think about it as a *book*. Scripture, though, is meant to be practiced. Whether we are reading by ourselves, with others, or it is being exposited for us, Scripture goes to work on our imaginations, drawing us into the story of God's people and allowing us to find our

---

7. Néstor O. Míguez, "The Old Creation in the New, the New Creation in the Old," *Wesleyan Perspectives on the New Creation*, ed. M. Douglas Meeks (Nashville: Kingswood Books, 2004), 70.

8. One excellent resource on prayer is William H. Willimon and Stanley Hauerwas, *Lord, Teach Us: The Lord's Prayer & the Christian Life* (Nashville: Abingdon Press, 2010). Another is Roberta Bondi's chapter "Praying the Lord's Prayer: Truthfulness, Intercessory Prayer, and Formation in Love" in *Liturgy and the Moral Self: Humanity at Full Stretch Before God* (Collegeville, MN: Liturgical Press, 1998).

own place in it. It sets the backdrop for the way we engage the world morally by setting our moral deliberations in the context of a world that has been created by a God who has pledged to remain faithful to this world throughout the work of it being made new.

Eucharist

We may not always see it, but gathering around the Lord's Table is an act of moral formation that tunes us to the way of the one who invites us to the feast and who has become the meal. We eat and drink a joy-filled feast at the gracious invitation of a God who is making the world new through a pattern of self-giving. When we go to the work of moral discernment, hopefully we won't be as resistant to decisions that align us with a crucified, self-giving Lord because we've been feasting at his table long enough to have become aligned with and accustomed to his pattern of sacrifice.

Baptism

Plunging under the waters of baptism and being raised to new life is the way Christians have historically viewed entrance into new life. Symbolizing death and resurrection, baptism is the entrance into a life lived in alignment with the new creation by grace. Each time we witness or participate in a baptism, we do it in the enduring hope that we are welcoming people into the space of new creation in the midst of the old.

"Questions concerning Christian ethics and the shape of the moral life cannot be adequately understood apart from thinking about how Christians worship," Don Saliers has argued.[9] Perhaps we can hold this in mind when we go about the work of our worship. What tools are we using in

---

9. Don Saliers, "Liturgy and Ethics: Some New Beginnings," *Journal of Religious Ethics*, vol. 7, no. 2 (Fall 1979).

our worship? How are we being shaped by the tools we use in worship? Joined together, the practices of worship and discernment open a place where we can begin to faithfully do the work of Christian ethics.

THREE | Working with Scripture

Our gaze now falls upon a beautifully intricate tool we have only considered briefly so far. In the work of Christian ethics, the Bible is both promising and complex. Because the promise compels us and the complexity calls for it, let's look at a few of the commitments that Christians—and Wesleyans in particular—make when it comes to Scripture.

First, God inspires Christian Scripture. While this phrase could mean a lot of different things, here we mean it to describe the reality that these texts came into being as a result of God moving with, in, and among the biblical writers. Because they flow from God's dynamic and active presence in the world, these texts carry the capacity to enliven and guide a Christian moral vision. The Spirit who illuminates our encounter with the text also opens new depths of understanding to us so we can continue to be empowered and transformed into God's faithful people.

Second, Scripture is faithful and can be trusted as a source for the work of Christian ethics. The long process of canonization (selecting the writings that would count as holy Scripture) bore out the early church's commitment to include only books that evidenced the Spirit's inspiration and were a faithful witness to what God had done and was doing. As Christian ethics looks to Scripture as a source, it does so by trusting that these texts have been chosen because they provide a faithful account of the way God acts and has continued to act.

This is why Christian Scripture is authoritative. Looking to Scripture as a source for the formation of Christian ethics is the act of placing ourselves under the authority of the way our ancestors saw God act. The Christian community is the one who gathers around these texts and affirms, "This is the witness of our ancestors who have seen God act. Its testimony carries authority among us! It shapes who we are!" The authority vested in these texts derives from its faithful witness to God's activity—a faithful witness made possible by the Holy Spirit's inspiration.

With these affirmations in place, we come to some of the complexities. First, the Bible is a library. While we join Wesley in being people "of one book," it's also important to recognize that Christian Scripture is a *collection* of multiple texts. Every book of the Bible has to be read on its own merit and allowed to speak to us on its own terms. Applying a one-size-fits-all method to Scripture will likely end up squeezing the life out of the Bible, rather than allowing it to draw us into its world, reorienting us to the pattern of God's new creation.

This acknowledgment calls the reader to have some amount of awareness about what *kind* of scripture they are reading. The Psalms, for example, will communicate differently than Revelation. To expect these two books to speak in the same way will lead us to miss the faithful witness given by each. This is not to say that some books are somehow *more* inspired or *less* truthful than others. Rather, it means we more fully allow the power of their inspiration to work on us when we receive them with the appropriate perspective. Like an apprentice in a workshop, our work will usually yield better results if we give ourselves the time to learn how to use the tools well and seek to be taught by those who have done this work before us across the years.[1]

The Story of (New) Creation

In the work of ethics, Scripture is not a collection of moral theories from on high but a set of inspired texts that offer us the grand story of God making and remaking the world. It is an epic saga, a narrative universe that has room for poetry, history, encouragement, and apocalypse. What we will do here, then, is briefly sketch the biblical saga with an eye toward the theme of new creation, looking for patterns and connections that allow us to enter the story.[2]

The saga opens by narrating the arena in which the story will take place. "In the beginning God created the heavens and the earth" (Gen. 1:1) are words that not only open the Bible but also set the stage for our understanding of the moral world. Leaving some of the more detailed points of creation for another chapter, what we should see here is the way heaven and earth are linked in this account. From the beginning, these two are meant to be together. They are distinct but not separate. Through thousands of years of philosophical influence tracing back to the likes of Socrates and Plato, modern people have tended to conceive of a world in which heaven and earth are held apart from one another. Heaven—the realm of God's presence, so to speak—is far above the realities of earth, and our eth-

---

1. Although Bible commentaries can be helpful in this regard, one single volume I've found useful in providing this overview is Gordon D. Fee and Douglas Stuart's *How to Read the Bible for All Its Worth*, 4th ed. (Grand Rapids: Zondervan Academic, 2014).

2. More detailed expositions of this type have been written, and I recommend them. Chief among those is Richard B. Hays, *The Moral Vision of the New Testament: A Contemporary Introduction to New Testament Ethics* (San Francisco: HarperSanFrancisco, 1996). Hays offers detailed strategies for reading Scripture for contemporary ethics and case studies ranging from abortion to ethnic conflict.

ics have developed accordingly. For Plato and the ancient Greek thinkers, the heavens were populated with goodness, and our task was to discern the pattern of goodness *in heaven*. The problem was that the eternal realm was so far away from the everyday realities of human life that the kind of discernment we needed had to be devoted to specialists called philosophers—who would dedicate their lives to discerning the inscrutable mysteries of goodness and truth that lived only in heaven.

When the modern era began to dawn, thinkers like Immanuel Kant chose to turn away from the heavens because, he thought, they were too far away and too uncertain to do us much moral good. The God of Christianity may live in the heavens, Kant conceded, but was so far removed from us that appealing to this God led to moral confusion or unprovable arguments. What we needed, Kant determined, was a moral theory that didn't rely upon God because the heavens in which this God resided were simply too far away. Kant wasn't the last to forge a theory like this. David Hume, John Stuart Mill, and John Rawls all have some version of this distance operating in their systems, all of which have been highly influential for the way their successors have approached ethics.

Genesis, however, knows nothing of this distance. The God who creates at the outset of the biblical drama isn't trying to hide or keep secrets. The arena of creation we find described in the Bible's opening chapters is the kind of construction project that has been customized for God to be *with* creation. Heaven and earth are two parts of one whole, and that whole is the arena of God and creation *together*. Woven into the theology of place, we find in Genesis a moral vision of the goodness of creation when creation and God live in close relationship. This is the reality that begins to disintegrate when the humans opt out of this closeness— yet another part of the story we'll need to wait to explore

Applying a one-size-fits-all method to Scripture will squeeze the life out of the Bible.

in more detail. In light of that disintegration, however, God seeks partnership with these humans for the sake of restoring the closeness. Whether it is Noah, Abraham and Sarah, or Moses, God covenants to stay close with them as they watch floodwaters rise and recede, await the birth of improbable babies, or wander in the wilderness in search of the promised land.

The humans whom God chooses to be God's partners are called to be "a kingdom of priests and a holy nation" (Exod. 19:6). As priests, they are called to mediate the nearness of God to a creation that has begun to operate as if the Creator is nowhere to be found. As a holy nation, they are called to be devoted to this God in their entirety. Their patterns, practices, and identity are meant to correspond to the God who has called them as covenant partners. These are the people who recall the arena of heaven and earth back together when they build the tabernacle—a place of God's nearness. These are the people who take that notion and apply it to a permanent dwelling place for God to be near the people. Solomon, the storied king who has the temple built, is supposed to be a king who serves the purpose of ordering things in a way that the goodness of God's nearness might be able to dwell with the people in the promised land, somewhere east of Eden. Politics are meant to establish the togetherness of heaven and earth. Kings are supposed to be caretakers of God's intentions.

Scripture isn't afraid to tell the stories of when and where those people fail in their work as priests, where kings enact their own agendas, and what it looks like to exchange the call to holiness for a story aligned with unholy purposes. As a moral document, the Bible doesn't present to us paragons of virtue on every page. Rather, it gives us an honest glimpse at the raw reality of humans who are called to partner with God but whom we often find sitting in the rubble of their own moral failures. It is the story of the hard struggle for new creation to take hold of a people who are imprisoned by old creation. It doesn't try to muffle the angry and sorrowful cries of the prophets, who beg their people to return to the kind of relationship with God that would make them a holy throwback to the heaven-and-earth goodness that was the garden of Eden.

In the midst of that struggle, the story turns to God's becoming flesh in the person of Jesus, who was the location of new creation coming into the old. In John's account, Jesus is the Word who actually *is* God and who "made his dwelling among us" (John 1:14). Translating John's words into English has diluted some of its significance; his language tells us that Jesus *tabernacles* in our presence, recalling the place of God's presence among the people of Israel. Heaven and earth are together yet again. Genesis is erupting into the present as God rebuilds the arena in Jesus. "Destroy this temple and I will raise it again in three days," John remembers Jesus saying (John 2:19). In him, heaven and earth touch, and a new possibility for life—the mark of what made the garden good—opens to us.

This is also the story of the way old creation played its trump card—death—in an attempt to squelch new creation. Had the old creation reality persisted unchanged, Jesus's story would have been yet another unremarkable chapter in the ongoing chronicle of history being written by those who most effectively employ violence and death. But his resurrection opened a place in the midst of old creation where that story no longer carried the day. The earliest versions of Mark's Gospel—the first of the four canonized Gospels to be written—conclude with the mystery of an empty tomb without giving any account of people actually encountering Jesus after his resurrection. Readers are left to wonder at that enigmatic emptiness—a place in the midst of the world where old creation's trump card has been robbed of its power.

The story of Scripture, then, tells the story of how Jesus's earliest followers started to proclaim the renewal of the world that began in an empty tomb. Their collective life together was a real-world outworking of new creation. Luke's account in Acts reads like a group of people who are getting up every day and walking into the reality of new creation without knowing entirely how it's happening. God's nearness is yet again the answer—this time in the presence of the Holy Spirit.

Paul's letters treat the new creation as fundamental for the kind of moral instruction he offers. These aren't the kinds of instructions that serve the purpose of propping up social norms or establishing a newer, stricter religious order. They are, rather, the kinds of things you would say to someone who is attempting to figure out how to live in the aftermath of a cataclysm. We can be reconciled to one another again, he tells the Corinthians. While old creation offers a host of ways to divide ourselves into opposing camps, "from now on we regard no one from a worldly point of view. Though we once regarded Christ in this way, we do so no longer. Therefore, if anyone is in Christ, the new creation has come: The old has gone, the new is here!" (2 Cor. 5:16–17). The moral question for the Corinthians— and, by extension, for us—is whether to live like this new creation is really here. "According to Paul, the death and resurrection of Jesus was an apocalyptic event that signaled the end of the old age and portended the beginning of the new."[3] The moral question is which age we find our lives aligned to now.

The bombastic, dazzling conclusion to Scripture's story in Revelation is the telescoping vision of history's future for those in the present—a larger-than-life reminder to people living in the midst of old creation that all things

---

3. Hays, *The Moral Vision of the New Testament*, 19.

are being made new according to the pattern of a crucified and resurrected Jesus. Ultimately, Revelation testifies, the way of Jesus really is the new creation, and the message we can receive now is that we ought to align ourselves with this way, even though it may be exceedingly hard. All other ways will slip into oblivion. Those who remain faithful to the way of Jesus will easily find a place in the New Jerusalem—the grand city in which heaven and earth are united once again forever. Revelation is a thoroughly ethical book. It forces us to ask ourselves: Is my life aligned to what will remain in the new creation or to what will disappear as all things are made new?

Finding Our Place in the New Creation Story

Richard Hays, a careful reader of Scripture for the sake of ethics, suggests we take the time to read Scripture on its own terms, which will allow Scripture's witness to land more convincingly, with all its sharp points and hard edges intact. "We can only read the texts carefully," he guides, "asking what common ground they share, what themes and images appear repeatedly, what convictions undergird their various stories and exhortations."[4]

A Wesleyan approach to Scripture will tune our interpretive frequencies to new creation's wavelength, and we may then be able to work with Scripture in a way that allows us to evaluate how a particular moral command in Scripture intersects with a contemporary moment. The way we might be able to approach Scripture for use in Christian ethics is through a *formational reflective dynamic*. In this approach, we appeal to Scripture in an attempt to find our place within its new creation story and let it speak to us about the alignment of our life toward new creation's ends. It is a dynamic of reading the texts, taking account of ourselves, and being

---

4. Hays, *The Moral Vision of the New Testament*, 189.

formed by what we find in the biblical story. We can measure ourselves against those texts, asking, "Do we reflect a new creation people well?" It's possible that such an encounter will reveal to us places where our lives can be amended, where we could be more faithful. Then we go into the world to act—to do our work. Returning time and again to encounter these inspired and living texts, we bring the work we have done and the people we have become in doing it, continually asking, "Have we become more faithful to the God who called us to be this kind of people?"

Adopting this approach allows Scripture to speak to us in evocative and authoritative ways. At the same time, it frees the Bible from having to act like a book of free-floating moral prescriptions, disconnected from place or history. It also prevents us from using Scripture in a way to simply toss verses back and forth at one another in a debate over moral prescriptions. As the faithful and authoritative testimony to God's actions, the Bible is a moral treasure, but when it is reduced to a series of moral sayings to stack up against one another in defense of a position, we risk strangling the life out of it.

In a formational reflective dynamic, we may read a passage written to a particular audience and see how that moral prescription is aligning the original hearers to be a new creation people. Then we may measure ourselves against their witness and ask, "How does this challenge us to align ourselves more faithfully to God's new creation project?" In this approach, we don't have to argue about whether the Levitical prescriptions on diet are less inspired than Jesus's teachings in the Sermon on the Mount. Both are inspired, and both speak powerfully, especially as we understand how each calls a people to be distinctly dedicated to God's purposes. Hays's ongoing advice is helpful here. After a careful and close reading of the individual texts, taking context into account, he recommends we begin testing that reading against others. "We proceed by trial and error," he says, taking what we find in a careful reading of one text and measuring it against the full range of possibilities we find in the rest of Scripture.[5]

When we take up Scripture with an eye toward Christian ethics, we do well to understand what we are reading, where it falls in the larger story, and what kind of role it plays in helping its audience understand its role in the new creation. The Bible's moral prescriptions aren't aimless. They point out certain issues in certain communities and guide them toward certain ends. Can we find ourselves reflected in them? Do we need to hear those commands too, to be able to become a people more fully aligned with God's new creation purposes? Could we be honest enough with ourselves to see the barriers to new creation at work in us as well, and could the prescriptions to them help us too?

Approaching Scripture this way allows us to use these sacred texts as a mirror and to ask whether we catch a glimpse of ourselves as we peer into its pages. As we stand before Scripture, are God's faithful people reflected back? Or do we recognize ourselves more in those who have opted to operate along the lines of old creation? Is the image we see there of those who have been responsive to the God who called a people to be caught up in God's ongoing work of redemption? Can we carry our work to the text and find it reflected back to us, or do we need to make an adjustment to who we are, how we respond, and how we are working?

5. Hays, *The Moral Vision of the New Testament*, 189. Hays provides a more detailed set of guidelines in his book.

FOUR

The Work of Discernment

When you lay Christian ethics alongside the great moral theories, its seeming lack of precision can be frustrating. Many of the moral philosophers devoted their lives to saying as precisely as they could how one should make moral decisions. Of course, Jesus was not one to muddle his message—at least in regard to his moral teachings. It doesn't get much clearer than, "Love your enemies and pray for those who persecute you" (Matt. 5:44). Still, there are times when we face moral decisions about things that Jesus never addressed directly during his ministry. The Gospel writers are silent on whether Jesus addressed biomedical ethics, end-of-life decisions, or the complex questions surrounding global economies.

It would be tempting for us, in the absence of some direct command by Jesus, to try to turn his teachings into principles that we could apply to a contemporary situation. When attempts to transform one of Jesus's moral teachings into a general principle, the sharp edges wear off, and it becomes a shadow of itself. "We should love everyone" isn't necessarily at odds with what Jesus said, but it's also a far cry from "Love your enemies." Our enemies have names. They have done very specific things that have hurt us in very particular ways. When someone has done something like that to me, I think it would be easier to lean toward the general principle of loving *everyone* in a vague sense of the word than to love *that* person who has done *this* thing to me.

If the commands of Jesus can't be turned into general principles, then what hope do we have of drawing them into contemporary life? As we've established, Wesleyan ethics aren't meant to apply to our lives in the same way we might apply a fresh coat of paint to the side of an old house. Wesleyan ethics wants to build an entirely new house. It wants to frame the entire structure, not coat the surface to give an appearance of newness that doesn't affect the foundation. What, then, do we do when we encounter a dilemma or question about which Jesus gave no direct instruction? Have we come to the limit of the usefulness of Jesus's moral teachings in a modern setting?

The work of *discernment* is one of the reasons we don't have to consign Jesus's moral teaching to the dustbin of history. Quite simply, discernment is the work disciples of Jesus do together when faced with an impending decision or moral dilemma. *Should I pursue this experimental medical treatment to combat a newly diagnosed disease? Should we adopt a child? What should we do for the children who show up at our church whose parents are addicted to drugs? Should we let this person teach a class at church?* In the midst of these particular, on-the-ground situations, moral principles would surely be easy to apply in a blanket sense. Blanket applications of moral principles, though—as anyone who gets into the trenches of compassionate ministry quickly learns—usually struggle to take account of the real lives of those we love.

Allen Verhey, a longtime teacher of Christian ethics, helps us catch the spirit of the way the earliest Christians did the work of discerning how their lives were to be lived, especially in pointing to the way these followers of Jesus "devoted themselves to the apostles' teaching" (Acts 2:42). These were not people enrolling in university courses taught in stately lecture halls by professors highly skilled in distilling complex ideas into a single presentation. No, the apostles were more likely telling stories about how Jesus dealt with on-the-ground situations concerning real people like them. "With people gathered in their work clothes, I imagine, Peter reminisced about an occasion on which Jesus had said this or that about life and the meaning of life, or about anxiety and the power to be carefree. Or, when some complained about the cheap, flashy woman who had joined their little assembly, John took five or six of the complainers aside to tell them about a long, hot, wearying walk the disciples took with Jesus one day just so Jesus could talk with just such a woman, a cheap Samaritan woman."[1] These were the kinds of communities that rose up around the idea that their way of life was first going to be guided by remembering what Jesus did in a particular situation and in light of that, ask, "What should we do *now*? How should we approach *this* situation while remembering what Jesus did?"

Though this approach may not be as neat and clean as some other approaches to ethics, the work of moral discernment in memory of Jesus is deeply committed to the good news of the gospel in *that* place. When communities of Christians take up this kind of work, they are bravely asking, "If everything we've been saying about Jesus is true, how can our action now be just as true?" We could also come at it this way: Christian faith is the trust that God is redeeming creation through Jesus Christ. The work of discernment is how we seek to align our action with what God is doing in Jesus to redeem creation and make it new.

Of course, this means that we are going to need to take our cues for what is *good* based on what God is doing in Jesus. "Good" can never be a generic word. If we are with a group of friends to discern a good path forward, that work will largely depend on coming to some kind of agreement on what the good is that our actions are aimed at achieving.

---

1. Allen Verhey, *Remembering Jesus: Christian Community, Scripture, and the Moral Life* (Grand Rapids: William B. Eerdmans Publishing Company, 2002), 9.

In my experience, the work of discernment in local church-es is increasingly difficult when the discernment partners have not thought through the vision of goodness that actu-ally guides them.

When communities of Christians come together to discern what they should do in a given situation, the partic-ular actions and words of Jesus really need to matter. This may seem incredibly obvious, but a focus on Jesus often fades into the distance when other concerns begin to arise: *Will this decision affect how much money the church receives? Will this decision help us attract more people to our communi-ty? Do we risk offending a longtime member who holds a strong opinion on this issue?* The work of discernment weighs these goods alongside one another and then proceeds when we think our actions are aimed at the highest good.

Doing the Work of Moral Discernment

We come now to the question you may have been asking for the past several pages: how do we do the work of discernment? Perhaps we have set our vision on Jesus's life and ministry as the highest good but are still struggling to see how his actions all those years ago can provide direct guidance to us now. What are the steps we can take to do this work?

I offer some suggestions that I hope will be helpful while also remembering Verhey's sage wisdom on the mat-ter: "There seems to be no recipe, nor is there any substi-tute, for the hard work of moral deliberation."[2] The pastoral and scholarly work I've done in Christian ethics gives me every reason to trust his statement. On one hand, I've rarely seen anything more beautiful than a group of diligent Jesus followers doing the hard work of asking how some situations should be handled. On the other hand, there

---

2. Verhey, *Remembering Jesus*, 13.

is also no clean-cut, how-to list when it comes to moral discernment. Every situation will be different, and every situation will call on us to prayerfully lean into the way of Jesus. While there is no one-size-fits-all approach to moral discernment, there is also no mistaking the remarkable thing that takes place when those who follow Jesus refuse to outsource their moral decisions to expedience or systems of retribution. As the way of Jesus is remembered well, that group begins to move in the world as the body of Christ.

With these challenges in mind, I offer this brief set of guidelines that may be helpful for beginning the work of moral discernment in the way of Jesus:

1) Begin with prayer, asking for wisdom, humility, and guidance. Pray the Lord's Prayer together, taking note of the emphasis on forgiveness and the reality that, even as the group perhaps deals with a situation of transgression, those who are gathered together also come to God seeking forgiveness for their own violations against others.

2) Take a few moments to remind the group of God's redemptive activity in the world to make all things new. Be reminded that the work of discerning a path forward is aimed at joining this situation to God's redemptive work. Consider yourselves agents and ministers of reconciliation (2 Cor. 5).

3) Have someone in the group—who has the capacity to step back and describe the situation well—write out the situation as best they can, describing the components that need the group's attention. Be as precise as possible with what exactly is known and what is merely conjecture. Have that person read back what they've written and ask the group if the account represents the situation faithfully.

4) Take some time to allow the members of the group to tell stories of Jesus's life and ministry that are

somewhat similar to what the group is discerning. Listen for the way those stories might allow you to remember Jesus in this situation.

5) Share with the rest of the group what you've heard in the story. Listen to others share their insights. Let them work on your imagination. Then ask, "What does it look like to be faithful to the way of Jesus in this situation?"

Whatever comes from processes like this, it's probably not going to be quick, cheap, or easy. The hope is that it *will* be faithful to the way God is acting in Jesus, and that will mean that it's *good*.

Moral Discernment in the Wesleyan Tradition

The practices of discernment in the Wesleyan tradition have long served the purpose of aligning our hearts with the work of new creation. When Wesleyans approach the work of discernment, it's not only that we are trying to make a decision on an issue but also that our decision will be the overflow of hearts that have been aligned toward new creation. The grand hope of the Wesleyan tradition is not that we become ethical people but that we become holy people whose ethics can do no other than reflect the image of God. Discernment, therefore, is not the quest to become more ethical but is the work of responding to the grace God pours out, and allowing our motivations, character, and imaginations to be transformed by and aligned toward God. The shape of the moral life in the Wesleyan tradition is a heart filled with the love of God that spills out into the work of love for our neighbor.

Over the years, Wesley saw that certain practices seemed to have the capacity to open one's heart to be filled more fully with love, to be taken more fully into deep relationship with the holy God who is near. The practices of visiting the sick, spending time with the poor, and bringing a bit of good news to those who had been imprisoned were, for Wesley, "means of grace" by which we open ourselves even more responsively to the grace that is renewing the image of God in us.

Alongside visiting the sick and caring for the poor, practices of discernment have been at home in the Wesleyan tradition from its beginning. While he was a university student at Oxford, Wesley gathered with a small group of people who sought to live lives of holiness. They prayed together, read Scripture, and committed to works of mercy, but they also ask themselves questions like, "Am I proud? Is there anyone whom I fear, dislike, disown, criticize, resent, or disregard?" In probing inquiries like these, the group opened themselves toward being prompted to walk the way of Jesus more faithfully.

Eventually, Wesley began establishing similar groups called band societies. These were small groups of people who "banded" together for the pursuit of Christlikeness. In their meetings they confessed to one another the temptations that pressed them and spoke honestly about the barriers that kept them from walking the way of Jesus. The level of transparency that characterized these meetings would make most of us uncomfortable today, but for those who were open to sharing their temptations and failures, it was a means of grace that helped them walk the way of Jesus more faithfully. The outcome was worth the discomfort.

These groups were organized under the conviction that we need the voices and insight of others who are also deeply committed to walking the way of Jesus to help us consider what we ought to do or to reflect on what we have done. Members were given space and time to reflect on their lives, to speak honestly about their obstructions and challenges, and to hear from one another about how their lives could conform more fully to the way of Jesus.

One of the most radical and socially subversive aspects of these groups was the way they banded together people from different social settings. In Wesley's day, the division between social groups and the power each group carried was stark. Wealthy factory owners would not have had much social contact with the people who worked in the factories they owned. If they were banded together, though, these groups opened the opportunity for those who held little social power or standing to speak into the life of a powerful person for the sake of walking the way of Jesus together.

When Methodism came to the United States, former slaves banded together with white landowners as equal partners on the path of the moral life—a nearly unthinkable reality for that time and place. Discerning together opened a space in which a formerly enslaved person could speak into the life of one who had previously held slaves, helping the socially powerful to walk the way of Jesus more faithfully. Factory workers could speak into the life of a factory owner with a holy challenge, encouraging them toward a life more aligned toward new creation. Because all the members of these groups agreed to this arrangement as they entered in, they opened themselves to be challenged, to grow, and to allow others to engage in the work of discernment with them.[3]

The more excellent way offers us a challenge to move our ethics beyond simply avoiding doing bad things, and toward opening ourselves to gathering with others for the work of discernment that not only helps us determine practical next steps but also shapes who we are becoming. It is a challenge to allow the voice of another person to say to us, "Here's where I see you walking faithfully. Here's where I see a misstep." It

---

3. For further exploration of Wesley's ministry breaking the rules of social convention, see Manfred Marquardt, *John Wesley's Social Ethics: Praxis and Principle,* trans. John E. Steely and W. Stephen Gunter (Nashville: Abingdon Press, 1992).

is a challenge to allow that kind of mutual discernment to help shape us into people who more readily open ourselves to God's love so that such infilling will splash out into the moral goodness of loving our neighbors. With that challenge in mind, I offer some suggestions on how that kind of work might be done. I'm drawing from Wesley's own approach, though I'm also allowing the influence of some of the work we've done on discernment to enter in.[4]

1) Find a group of people who are committed to doing this kind of work for the sake of growth and formation. This kind of work isn't about solving problems so much as it is about growth in grace. The aim of all this work is to live more fully into the redemptive rhythms of grace and to be renewed in the image of God. Originally, these groups came together to confess their faults to one another and pray for one another, that they should be healed. If the entire group is committed to that outcome, it will probably keep the conversation moving in the same general direction. Wesley organized men with men and women with women into groups of about twelve, which may create an atmosphere of openness, challenge, and honesty.

2) Make sure those of different social settings are included. A host of different voices will help to peel back cultural and social blinders.

3) Wesley suggested opening and closing each meeting with prayer, and coming with an expectation that each person was willing to share honestly,

---

4. Specifically, these suggestions are drawn from "The Rules of the Band Societies" that Wesley wrote in 1738. See Wesley, *Works*, 4:272–73. Additionally, I recommend Kevin M. Watson and Scott Thomas Kisker, *The Band Meeting: Rediscovering Relational Discipleship in Transformational Community* (Franklin, TN: Seedbed Publishing, 2017).

including temptations they've faced since the previous meeting.

4) Before anyone joins the group, they should know what they are getting into. Wesley proposed asking them honest questions like, "Is the love of God filling your heart? Are you willing to hear from others, even about your faults? Are you willing to be honest with the group about your motivations and struggles?"

5) Each meeting, Wesley proposed, should be centered around four distinct questions: What sins have you committed since our last meeting? What temptations have you faced? How were you delivered? What have you thought, said, or done, of which you doubt whether it be sin?

Obviously, this isn't the kind of discernment work that can be undertaken casually or lightly, but it is the kind of work that opens a path toward moral formation. It's the kind of hard work that goes beyond delivering an answer to "What should I do?" and gets at the deeper question, "Am I a person who reflects the image of God?" That second question will undoubtedly flow into all aspects of life. It is a glimpse of the moral life that is less about figuring out how to solve an isolated ethical problem and more about becoming a person of holy virtue whose whole life moves in rhythm with the way God is making all things new through Jesus.

FIVE

Working with a Limp
Divine Encounter and Holiness Ethics

The nation of Israel got its name in the dark of night along the banks of a river. There, a conniving patriarch picked up the same pattern he'd known since childhood and did whatever he needed to do to get a blessing. "I will not let you go unless you bless me," Jacob said to a mysterious adversary with whom he had wrestled all night (Gen. 32:26). When it was all said and done, Jacob came limping away from what he called an encounter with God. "I saw God face to face, and yet my life was spared," he would go on to say (v. 30). His out-of-joint hip socket was a testimony to his new name: "Your name will no longer be Jacob, but Israel, because you have struggled with God" (v. 28). A face-to-face encounter with God that left Jacob limping shaped Israel's imagination of itself. Taking the name of God-wrestlers, they are the ones who come away from encounters with God blessed with a limp.

Doing the work of Christian ethics with a limp hardly seems like something we should aspire to, but the story of Jacob wrestling with God sets a moral motif that can be incredibly helpful to communities seeking a faithful path forward in the face of daunting moral challenges. As I hear often, the church is "wrestling" with lots of large issues. In the process, communities often seek to make statements or rules to address these issues. How do communities formulate those rules? What role should rules play in Christian communities?

Often, rules emerge as communities wrestle with specific situations that arise. I received a message recently from a seminary where I teach, mandating that online students could no longer participate in videoconference classes while in their cars. The first thing I thought was that such a rule didn't come out of thin air—that rule must have been written because someone had been driving during class. While it's perfectly natural to the life of a community to work this way, this dynamic often comes with a shadow side.

Sometimes communities respond to situations that arise in a given moment, and over time, we collect rules and guidelines that were meant to respond to particular situations at particular times but don't work together as a whole. For example, if a majority of our population begins to take trains or ride in self-driving cars, should we still prohibit students from attending a videoconference class during their commute? Do we create a new rule? Should we amend or abolish the current rule? The point is that our rules can quickly become more like an odd collection of ethical knickknacks rather than an overarching way to help a community align its life to God's new creation. Obviously, we can't take every type of community into consideration here. This is a book, after all, on Christian ethics in the Wesleyan tradition, so it would be best for us to focus there, and especially on what distinguishes a *Wesleyan* approach to Christian ethics. The primary focus that calls Wesleyans to think through what they do is *holiness*.

What Difference Does Holiness Make?

"Holiness" is a loaded word, especially when it's spoken in relationship to ethics. For some, it has been used to divide the world into the things we do and the things we don't do. For others, it's a signifier of a certain style of dress. For many, though, the word probably rings a bit hollow, a kind of rhetorical relic of religious yesteryear.

There isn't a singular description of holiness that can do it justice. The angle by which we'll approach it here is to point out that holiness is a way of describing *difference*. As holy, God is completely and utterly *different* from anything in the created world, and also different from all of the other gods that Israel's neighbors worship. In the ancient Near East, religious life usually ran along the lines of worshiping as many gods as possible because each of them could do something different for you. When a single God above all gods shows up in the form of a burning bush, telling Moses that the ground upon which he stands is holy, we begin to sense that we aren't dealing with a god who simply handles all burning bushes—but a God who handles all things.

Worshiping that God makes Israel strange. It is odd to worship only one God. It is even stranger to arrange all of one's life around the one God, but that is precisely what Israel does. Early on in Israel's story, this holy God calls a people to be holy so that, through them, God can bless the world (Exod. 19:6). Their response is to live a life of devotion to that God. For our Israelite ancestors, their lived holiness is what makes them a distinct people in the world. To live in a dedicated way to *one* God, who has asked them to exhibit behaviors and patterns of life that make them oddly identifiable among their neighbors, who tend to worship a number of gods, is vital to their identity as a people.

Their ethics cannot be separated from their identity; they do *these* things because they have entered into a covenant with *this* God. Our God-wrestling predecessors signal that they are grappling with someone who is completely different from the gods of their neighbors by the way they live in a completely different way. What they eat, whom they marry, and the things they do to care for one another are all connected to their commitment to the fact that their God is absolutely different. Their God is *holy*.

As a way of pointing to God's utter difference and living in response to that holy God, Christians have sometimes chosen to remain distinct in their life's work and practice. Often, notions of purity are held up as an ethical standard in this moral approach. Maintaining one's purity by refusing to partake in certain actions and behaviors is seen not only as a way of remaining true to the God who has called us but sometimes also as being connected to living a life that is pleasing to God. Born out of a desire to embody an ethics that points to God's holiness, there is an undeniable temptation toward legalism that has lurked around the edges of these movements. Although remaining faithful to God calls for vital devotion, notions of what is pure and impure can often be codified in this approach so that one who somehow wills herself to do only the "pure" things and avoid the "impure" things can be counted as "holy."[1] Holiness ethics in this mode can all too easily be reduced to a set of rules. Once we've taken that step, those who are most successful at living according to those rules are faced with the secondary temptation to walk intrepidly into the future, firm in the knowledge that they have done the right thing.

In what I am proposing, though, holiness ethics is the limp that marks the people who have wrestled with God. Christian ethics is the way we walk after an encounter with the living and holy God. A holy people don't do their ethical

---

1. Richard Beck's warning is to work carefully around the categories of purity and holiness. If something is impure, it tends to trigger a psychological response of disgust, toward both actions and actors. He recommends we handle purity language with a hazmat suit, understanding that it can quickly become toxic. But if holiness is conceived not as a boundary marker of the pure against the impure but as a defining mark of people who have come close to the purifying fire of God and walked away with singed lips, we can put the hazmat suit away and call people close to this God whose very nature will be the agent of transformation. See Richard Beck, *Unclean: Meditations on Purity, Hospitality, and Mortality* (Eugene, OR: Cascade Books, 2011).

work with a heroic and flawless gait. Their walk has the distinctive trait of those who have wrestled with God, embracing a strength seen in humility and power made perfect in weakness. If we think that coming away from a wrestling match with God will leave us triumphantly marching away, we have misunderstood the kind of ethics that results from an encounter with holiness. This is why holiness ethics cannot truly be codified as a legalistic list of do's and don'ts, especially when it's held apart from an encounter with the living God.

If our attention turns to *what* we do before it turns toward *who* informs what we do, we have already taken a misstep on our path toward Christian ethics in the light of holiness. The Israelites—the people who are called to be holy—remind themselves of this time and again. The stories at the core of their identity are reminders that the God who encountered them has done so in ways we could not have expected. Israel's prophets call out to the people over and over again to remember that simply doing things apart from God is not the way holy people live. "I hate, I despise your religious festivals; your assemblies are a stench to me," Amos memorably quotes the Lord as saying (Amos 5:21). This charge is set in the context of God's plea to Israel: "Seek me and live" (Amos 5:4). As the chapter unfolds, God's list of Israel's moral missteps comes down to this: *you've stopped seeking me and have gone your own way.* Even the festivals—though originally meant to celebrate Israel's encounters with God—have become morally bankrupt because they are no longer about seeking encounter with the living God. The words of the prophet are a helpful challenge to any community called to holiness. When our principles are upheld for their own sake, apart from a vital encounter with the living God, we run the risk of turning our ethics into an idol and engaging in the triumphal march of those who have never wrestled with God.

Holiness ethics is what happens when a person is transformed by the love of God.

My point is that one of the most distinctive aspects of Christian ethics is that it tends to be an ethics that is worked out in *response* to a God who has captured our imagination. We shouldn't miss the radical nature of what this means. The work of Christian ethics isn't the attempt to align ourselves with some unmovable and distant set of eternal principles; it is the lived response to a living God who is making all things new in a dynamic way. This God became flesh, dwelt with us, and called us to follow in his way. Holiness ethics is a lived response empowered by God's ongoing, active presence with us. This ethics requires active relationship with the God who calls us, claims us, and empowers us for response. If we stop for a moment to consider this reality, we can see a world of thrilling moral possibility.

What Does Athens Have to Do With Sinai?

In the earliest days of the Christian faith, an influential thinker set pen to paper with the purpose of not only explaining the new Christian movement to its critics but also to prevent believers from falling into the trap of heresy. In making his case, Tertullian set the Christian faith apart from Greek philosophy, which he called "the material of the world's wisdom."[2] "What indeed does Athens to do with Jerusalem?" he asked. His rhetorical question was meant to press to Christians the question of whether their lives should be shaped by the philosophy of teachers like Plato and Aristotle, or according to the tradition that was passed down to them through Israel.

Athens was the seat of philosophical teaching. The great masters—Socrates, Plato, and Aristotle—made Athens their home, and it was the place to go for anyone who was

---

2. Tertullian, "On Prescriptions against Heretics" in *Ante-Nicene Fathers*, ed. Alexander Roberts and James Donaldson (Peabody, MA: Hendrickson Publishers, 2004), 3:246.

serious about studying the truth of life. Tertullian presented an alternative vision for the good life. Jerusalem, he said, was where Christians ought to look because it was where God's presence dwelt in the temple and where Jesus was crucified and resurrected. "Our instruction comes from 'the porch of Solomon,'" he said, "who himself taught that 'the Lord should be sought in the simplicity of heart.'"[3]

I'm going to take a step back from Tertullian's famous question and ask instead about Sinai. It is the distinction between Athens, the school at the heart of a bustling city, and Sinai, the far-flung hilltop in the middle of nowhere, where a group of newly freed slaves with training in little more than making bricks came to encounter a holy God. This is not to say philosophy should be excluded from the work of Christian ethics. It is to raise the question of *how* we go about working the moral life. Athens represents the method by which we reason our way to moral *principles*. Sinai is the place where Israel encounters a holy and living God, and comes away from that encounter faced with the question of how they ought to live in response. They are grasped by a relationship and enter into covenant, rather than a set of principles, with a living God. They are named for the limp in their walk, a blessing given to them from their ongoing wrestling match with a living God (Gen. 32).

As compelling as some of the theories of the Western tradition have been, the common thread that tends to unite them is that they present ideas and then ask how we align ourselves to those ideas. Plato's world of eternal Ideas was precisely that: ideas. If the old adage is true that Western philosophy is a series of footnotes to Plato, an idea-based ethics is baked into the philosophical tradition, including the way we tend to envision ethics. A Christian ethics of holiness reaches beyond some of those resources. Its start-

---

3. Tertullian, "Against Heretics," 3:246.

ing point is not as much in the Academy of Athens, but at the base of Mount Sinai and the foot of the cross. Given the choice between Socrates and Moses, it tends toward the man who responded to the call of a holy God, rather than the teacher who attempts to reason his way to a pure idea.

When I talk with groups who are attempting to discern a path forward around a moral issue, most tend to *reason* their way to a rule based on a principle. Fairness, kindness, legality, or some other standard is assumed to be capable of bearing the moral weight of the decision in front of them. What fascinates me, though, is how rarely an encounter with a holy God tends to shape the conversation, even among holiness communities. This is not to say Christian ethics should turn away from the resources of Western philosophy entirely, but it does raise the question of how much more comfortable holiness communities are in turning toward the reasonable principles worked out in the halls of Athens, rather than the encounter with the holy God that took place at Sinai.

Remembering Sinai is central to Israel's moral life, and it is central to any Christian ethics concerned with holiness. To remember Sinai is to acknowledge that holiness ethics cannot be reasoned out at a safe distance from encounter with a holy God. Holiness ethics is not a list of moral prescriptions that happen to fit a "conservative" or "activist" or some other principled description of life. Rather, holiness ethics is how a people who have encountered a holy God work out their call to be holy. Significantly, the immediate outcome of the encounter with the beauty of holiness at Sinai is a moral one: God gives the ten ethical sayings.[4]

---

4. Typically, these "sayings" are known as the Ten Commandments. A close examination of the text, however, shows that "commandment" really isn't part of the text. Our term "Ten Commandments" is usually a subheading that modern editors have added to our Bibles to show us where this story can be found. The Hebrew word in the passage, *dabar,* is a fairly general term for a speech, or a

In fact, the transition between Exodus 19's account of this holy encounter and God's speaking of the ten moral instructions is quite thin. As soon as the splendorous scene of God's mountaintop descent concludes, the text lurches into moral admonition.

Equally significant is the relationship we see between encounter and admonition. Following the pattern of Israel's encounter with a holy God at the far side of the wilderness, there is *first* an encounter with the living God, and *then* there is the offering of the tenfold description of the holy life. *First*, Israel comes undone when they see the holiness of God, shaken by a bone-rattling encounter with what Rudolf Otto calls "the numinous," a word he invented to describe a meeting with holiness.[5] *Then* the Lord offers Israel a way to live in response: a code.

And here we come face to face with a moral reality that cannot be ignored if we are to do Christian ethics with holiness in mind: whatever kind of moral vision the people developed during their time in Egypt, the vision of holiness they encounter challenges it, and a new moral vision is gifted to them on the other side of that encounter. Egypt had its own moral vision, no doubt, its own way of naming things "good." That vision undoubtedly went to work on Israel's imagination since Israel lived there for four centuries. But when we come to a holy God with all of our moral categories neatly arranged and our moral vision already formed, do

word that has been spoken. Sometimes it is translated as "command," but it can just as easily be translated "message." In the same way that "word" in English can come to mean different things depending on context, *dabar* comes to our eyes through the lens of the kind of word that is spoken in the text. The point is that it doesn't *always* or even naturally mean "command." Hebrew has a word for "command"—*mitzvah*—but that word isn't used here. The encounter with God is primary, and the things God says to Israel afterward are instructive of how to live in light of such an encounter. They are not commands that have moral meaning apart from the encounter with the God who issued them.

5. Rudolf Otto, *The Idea of the Holy*, trans. John W. Harvey (London: Oxford University Press, 1923).

we really expect to walk away with those categories undisturbed or our moral vision unchallenged? Holiness ethics, if it is going to be holiness ethics at all, will rouse us from our usual. It will disrupt the moral vision we've been lulled into accepting, and confront us with one that shakes us free to be entirely devoted to God's new creation.

The ten "words" God speaks describe what life lived in response to God's holiness looks like. These sayings live in a kind of spiraling relationship with the people. The words are spoken as the description of lives lived in dedication to God, the people live into the description, their lives become more devoted to God, and so on. The moral point is that rigid and willful adherence to the ten sayings of God is not the moral vision that shapes holiness ethics. Rather, a people's living encounter with a holy God will shape them into and empower them to be a kind of people who won't murder, commit adultery, or steal—*all because they will have no other gods before the living, holy God*. Other gods can't possibly shape that kind of people because any other god is not holy.

Limping away from Legalism

In holiness ethics, whatever ethical codes and guidelines we might draft are intended to be a descriptive and helpful *response.* Codes in themselves cannot be holy if they are divorced from the action of the One who is holy. When codes and rules are written to preserve and establish social norms for their own sake, they run the immediate risk of becoming gods we have erected before the living and holy God.

The holiness codes of Israel are intended to allow them the freedom to live in complete devotion to the God who has called them to be holy. These codes serve the purpose of setting a people apart to bear witness to the world without being ensnared in old creation's patterns and shaped by its moral imagination. When people begin to serve the codes themselves, however, they run the risk of fashioning the means of their freedom into the chains of moral captivity. "Let my people go!" is a calling to develop a moral imagination that responds to and serves God's redemptive purposes in the world. It is the command to set a people free to live an ethics of new creation.

If those codes become descriptive of the moral response to divine encounter, the possibility opens for them to be morally formative. To hearken back to Wesley, divine action and encounter come first, and the secondary response is to ask, "What does it look like to live in faithful response to what we have encountered?" The answers to that question may emerge in the form of guidelines, codes, and laws, but those guidelines do not ask us to serve *them*. An ethics built on serving the codes themselves short-circuits the beautiful possibilities for holiness and relegates us to the idolatry that the responsive law of Moses is meant to overturn. When those codes become a means of response to the encounter with a holy God, they are serving a holy purpose beyond themselves.[6]

---

6. The Church of the Nazarene's *Manual* contains a section called The Covenant of Christian Conduct, which is the primary code of ethics for the denomination. The items contained in that code, however, are described in the covenant as "guides and helps to holy living" (46). Wisely, the authors of this introductory remark have identified the covenant not as a punitive list of rules but as a means of grace that arises in response to the gracious operation of a holy God. The covenant also recognizes the limits of codes of conduct in the holy life. Acknowledging that no catalogue of moral behavior can address all issues, readers are prompted to "earnestly seek the aid of the Spirit in cultivating a sensitivity to evil that transcends the mere letter of the law" (47). In this gesture is an implicit recognition that the Spirit's work is primary and ought to be treated as such. The resulting code ought to be considered seriously as a help and guide, rather than treated as the key to the holy life, or wielded as a type of gatekeeping mandate aimed at moral behaviors. The theology of the Holiness tradition celebrates freedom from those behaviors but humbly acknowledges that such freedom is a gift of God, resulting from the Spirit-filled life. "The church joyfully proclaims the good news that we may be delivered from all sin to a new life in Christ" (46). See Church of the Nazarene, *Manual: 2017–2021* (Kansas City, MO: Nazarene Publishing House, 2017).

Reminding us that John Wesley's view of the holy life was the human heart filled with love for God and neighbor, transforming us and reorienting our desires and motivations, a generation of Wesleyan theologians have gestured toward an ethics that is the *secondary result* of God filling us with love.[7] Holiness ethics, they have prophetically reminded us, is what happens when a person is transformed by the love of God. Rather than rigidly adhering to a set of laws or even demanding that others do so, we come to trust that our encounter with holy love will transform our motivations such that we won't *want* to do things that breach the relationship we have with God and neighbor. Like our Israelite ancestors, Wesleyans hopefully see that encounter with God is the primary moral reality, while the ethical codes that result—important as they are—flow secondarily from the primary reality. When that dynamic is reversed, a legalistic form of idolatry—moralism—is not far behind.

This is not to say that the holy life is simply the absence of moral standards. Israel's call to holiness at Sinai comes with moral instructions that aid them in being a people who are set apart for God's redemptive purposes. During his life, John Wesley was charged with being an "antinomian," a term used to describe one who is opposed to norms, rules, or standards. Wesley responded that moral standards were not to be ignored but insisted that we understand the role rules play in the new creation dynamic of grace. Like Israel at Sinai, the moral boundaries are a means of living faithfully unto God, but we aren't called to live unto the rules themselves. Good works are to be the evidence of a life transformed by God's grace. "God loves you: therefore love and obey him," Wesley wrote in 1751. "Christ died for you: therefore die to sin. Christ is risen: therefore

7. See, for example, Mildred Bangs Wynkoop, *A Theology of Love*, 2nd ed. (Kansas City, MO: Beacon Hill Press of Kansas City, 2015).

rise in the image of God. Christ liveth evermore: therefore live to God, till you live with him in glory."[8] A life lived toward goodness is a *response* to God's grace, rather than the requirement for receiving God's grace.

In a Wesleyan vision of ethics, the good life is nothing other than a gift granted to us by God, empowered by the Holy Spirit. It is not that rules and codes have no place in a Wesleyan ethics but that such codes serve the purpose of freeing people to live into God's redemptive purposes. Guidelines, while not necessarily bad, find their place in the life-giving dynamics of Christian ethics when they flow from God's sanctifying presence and when they serve to free people to live the good life of joining God's new creation work. It is not associating more closely with rules that makes us holy; only association with the holy God can do that. Neither is the holy life found in throwing aside all discipline and guidance in the name of liberty. In the life of God's people, rules and codes serve to free us but must be recognized for what they are when they cease to serve God's new creation purposes.

This is all part of the wrestling match of divine encounter. The limp that is the gift to a holy people is also our continual reminder that our own rules may need to be wrestled away from us when we begin to serve them. A holiness ethics will always need to retain the possibility that God may need to free us from our own codes, and we may not be willing to relent. In the economy of God's new creation, though, freedom will probably also come with a limp, the mark of those who walk and work as people who met God along the banks of a river and came away forever changed.

---

8. Wesley, "Of Preaching Christ," in *John Wesley*, ed. Albert C. Outler (London: Oxford University Press, 1980), 237.

SIX

The Work of Love in the Created Order

The work of Christian ethics shares an intimate relationship with the work God does in creating. We hear only a few words of Scripture before we are introduced to a God who *works*. The distant God, removed from and floating above the beauty, challenge, grit, and grime of life in the created order is nowhere to be found in Genesis 1–2. The God of Genesis 2 works in the dirt of the ground, gathering it together and breathing life into it. It is none other than God who planted a garden in which the humans would come to dwell (Gen. 2:8). Whatever else we can say about the theological message Genesis 1–2 sends, this much is clear: God is working and active. When it comes to the humans we see in that same passage, this much is also clear: God has invited them to work too.[1] From the thoughtful, imaginative work of naming animals to the earth-bound effort of caring for a garden, God calls humanity to join in the work of creation (Gen 2:15–19).

The work God calls for is the kind that happens with a joyful sense of gratitude. This work is not ceaseless toil; it also includes delighted rest. The Sabbath rest God participates in and calls humans to join is the ongoing reminder

---

1. Though many English translations of Genesis 2:8 say "man," the Hebrew word used to describe the human being does not carry the same gendered connotation that the term *ish*—used to describe a male human—does. Until the arrival of the *ishah* (woman), the word for a human being is *adam*, signaling that this being was made out of dirt (*adamah*).

that this work is not the endless means of raw production. Sabbath reminds us that work is not aimed at a good called production. Our work finds its good and joyful rhythm when it reflects the loving work God has done in creating.

Sabbath also serves to break the temptation we have to make creation into a construction project under our control. While humans have work to do in creation, it comes at the invitation of the God who says, "Let there be . . .". The world in which we work is God's world, and we are graciously invited to join in the work of creation. How, then, should we go about doing this work? What can we learn from the doctrine of creation—especially as it lives in the Wesleyan tradition—about how we might do the work of Christian ethics?

Compassion on All He Has Made

The words of Psalm 145 were some of John Wesley's favorite. "The Lord is good to all; he has compassion on all he has made. All your works praise you, Lord; your faithful people extol you" (vv. 9–10). In this biblical song of praise, the close relationship between God's works and God's love is unmistakable. The God who has created this world, working to bring it into existence, is the same God who faithfully loves all of it. For some of us, a more obvious sentence has never been written, but this has not always been the way humans have understood the world in relationship to the divine. At points throughout human history, the gods some cultures worshiped have been understood to be at work in the world—but not always for the sake of love.[2] That the God of Israel created the world *and* loves it is a

---

2. The early Greeks, for example, adopted notions of morality from the epic poems of Homer, whose works told the stories of gods who were "vastly more powerful and knowing than man, yet not particularly moral." See Eugene Garrett Bewkes and James Calvin Keene, *The Western Heritage of Faith and Reason* (New York: Harper & Row, 1963), 219–21.

fairly novel affirmation in the ancient world. Passages like Psalm 145 and the opening chapters of Genesis speak "as a testimony to the God who is love."[3]

The beauty we encounter here goes deeper when we also see that God's work and God's love share a relationship that is too close to separate one from the other. Work, as we often imagine it, impinges on our freedom and takes us away from those we love. "I wish I could go with you to dinner," we might say to a friend, "but I have to work." God's work, however, is nothing other than the activity of holy love. God's work is what holy love looks like in action. God does not work in spite of love; God's work is the superabundant overflow of love. If God's character and nature are love, the work of creation is what naturally happens. Creation happened because God is love. I say all of this not only to relish in the beauty of divine love but also to make the point that God's work of creation allows love to work freely. The way God has formed creation allows love to thrive. There's nothing more natural to God's creation than for the created order to live freely in love. Not only is the divine work of creation an act of love, but the workmanship exhibited in creation also testifies to the Creator, whose nature and name are love.[4]

Often, the language we use to describe this loving workmanship is "order." God has not only spoken creation into existence but has also ordered it in such a way that the whole creation might come to know and experience God's love. Creation is the arena that God has lovingly crafted in which love might give life and where that life might be extended to one another as acts of love. If this arena is to

---

3. Michael E. Lodahl, *The God of Nature and of Grace: Reading the World in a Wesleyan Way* (Nashville: Kingswood Books, 2003), 56.

4. See Charles Wesley's hymn "Come, O Thou Traveler Unknown," *The United Methodist Hymnal* (Nashville: The United Methodist Publishing House, 1989), #386.

function well, it has to be ordered. The opening lines of Genesis tell us that "the earth was formless and empty, darkness was over the surface of the deep" (1:2). This foreboding image signals a lack of capacity for love to flourish. The chaos that characterized the primordial cosmos did not allow for lovingly gifted life to grow until an ordering word was spoken. "Let there be" is the word-work of love. The Creator separates light from dark, day from night, and land from sea—all for the sake of ordering creation in such a way that life can be received as the work of love and that work might continue among the created order.

To the creatures made in God's image, we hear the divine command spoken: "Be fruitful and increase in number; fill the earth and subdue it" (Gen. 1:28). These human creatures, made male and female (v. 27), are meant to fill the earth and to join in the creative work of ordering it for love. Bearing God's image, they are to fill the earth with the divine likeness and "subdue" it. The work of subduing is nothing other than the work of love. It is joining in God's creative work of ordering creation in such a way that love can flourish. To interpret the divine command to subdue the earth as permission to take possession of creation's resources in such a way that God's creation is harmed or love is blocked is a violation of humanity's mandate. Subduing here is meant for freedom in love—not for subjection, misuse, abuse, or oppression. As those invited into the creative dynamic of a loving God, humans are the ones who have been gifted with the capacity to subdue creation, but the misuse of that capacity signals humanity's moral agency that can be—and has been—abused, which stifles love, rather than allowing it to flourish freely.[5] The work

---

5. The Hebrew word being used here (*kabash*) is often used in the Old Testament to describe Israel's work of subduing the land (Num. 32; Josh. 18). When this word is used in an oppressive sense, it results in an outcry from the people, as in Nehemiah 5: "Although we are of the same flesh and blood as

of subduing is meant to be aimed at showing compassion toward all God has made. When humans do this well, we more fully reflect the image of our Creator.

"When God created the heavens and the earth," Wesley reminds us, "at the conclusion of each day's work it was said, 'And God saw that it was good.'"[6] The goodness of the creation, Wesley continues, can be seen in three characteristics. First, everything God created was "suited to the end for which it was designed." Second, everything made by God "adapted to promote the good of the whole," and finally, all that was made prompted "the glory of the great Creator."[7] For Wesley, it was not enough to simply affirm that God created all that there is. Going further, he asserted that God had made creation in *this* way so that, in the order of creation, every creature could flourish, that flourishing would be mutually beneficial to the rest of creation, and all of that would bring praise to God.

Already we are beginning to pick up hints about the way we might do the work of Christian ethics in light of creation. The work we are called to do and the life we are called to truthfully live is one that joins the order of God's good creation rather than departing from it. It is to work toward the end for which we were created, to do our work in a way that it is mutually beneficial to the rest of creation, and to do our work for God's glory. To do our work like this is not only to live into the dynamics of the created order, but

---

our fellow Jews and though our children are as good as theirs, yet we have to subject [*kabash*] our sons and daughters to slavery. Some of our daughters have already been enslaved [*kabash*], but we are powerless, because our fields and our vineyards belong to others" (v. 5). The work of subduing can be in service to the flourishing of love, or it can be in service to the dismantling of the created order. Vindication arises from God when the prophet Micah envisions God using the power of *kabash* to subdue Israel's misuse of *kabash* for oppressive purposes: "You will again have compassion on us; you will tread [*kabash*] our sins underfoot and hurl all our iniquities into the depths of the sea" (7:19).

6. Wesley, "God's Approbation of His Works," *Works*, 2:206.

7. Wesley, "God's Approbation of His Works," 206.

it is also to make our lives the truthful "amen" in response to the divine proclamation about this ordered creation: "It is good."

What Are Humans That You Are Mindful of Them?

Stepping back for a moment to consider why the Christian faith has a doctrine of creation at all, we might be puzzled. Why does a religious movement need an origin story? When it comes to Christian faith in particular, why have Christians held so adamantly to a narrative about the world coming into existence? What is the doctrine of creation *for*?

The way we answer these questions is morally significant. If the doctrine of creation is for proving a timeline of creation over against natural science, our ethics will surely follow. It will become a tool in our hand to prove a point. If the doctrine of creation instead serves to help us understand who we are, a different world of moral possibility opens to us. The story that Christian Scripture wants to tell about creation gives us a narrative in which we *find* ourselves. The opening chapters of Genesis want to tell a story about God's creative endeavors, in part to remind us who *we* are in relationship to the God who created. We often use the term "contingent" (dependent) to describe the kind of relationship this story narrates. We are beings, Genesis reminds us, who rely and depend on God's gracious, creative, and sustaining activity.

There are at least two distinct ways in which contingency is working in this text. First, there is a sense of *ontological* contingency. "Ontological" is a technical term that refers to the nature of being—what something *is*. Behind the term "ontological contingency" is the notion that we receive our life and our being from God. We do not make ourselves or give life to ourselves; rather, we receive our lives as a gift at every moment. Our every breath is a gift from the Creator, and we depend on God's creative work for our next breath. We are beings of dust who would quickly return to dust were it not for the enlivening, sustaining breath that comes from outside ourselves. God's loving, gracious breath gives us life: "For in him we live and move and have our being" (Acts 17:28a).

The second sense in which we are contingent draws most of our attention. It is what I refer to as "moral contingency." In the same way we receive our life from God, so too do we receive our moral context. The message of moral contingency rings out in the opening chapters of Genesis, saying, *This is the world God has created, and we have been placed within it. Our role as human beings is not to shape the world into our image but to image God to this world. To find ourselves in that order is to freely flourish within the world God has created.* In a modern world, this message rarely finds a receptive audience. The philosophical air we breathe as modern people is pungently laden with the idea that we are not contingent upon anything or anyone and that the good life is one we have hewn ourselves from the stone of contemporary society.

Consider the lyrics of some of the most popular film soundtracks produced in late modernity. The hit movie soundtrack that kids sang while watching *UglyDolls* put these lyrics on their lips: "You define yourself/You and no one else." To draw a song from another cultural moment, in Disney's *Frozen* the heroine Elsa sings, "It's time to see what I can do/To test the limits and break through/No right, no wrong, no rules for me, I'm free!" And scores of people learned to sing along to the melodious ballad "A Million Dreams" from *The Greatest Showman* "I don't care, I don't care, so call me crazy/We can live in a world that we design/I think of what the world could be/A vision of the one I see/A million dreams is all it's gonna take/A million dreams for the world we're gonna make."

Most of the time, the philosophy or theology shaping our moral imagination isn't coming to us from textbooks or lectures. We sing it in our cars, we entertain ourselves with it in our living rooms, and we internalize it through hundreds of small encounters with the kinds of songs I've quoted above and the hundreds that have been written since. If we were to take a quick account of those encounters, we might see there is a moral imagination being shaped in the way we understand ourselves in relationship to creation: *I am a self-made being, there should be nothing beyond my own desires to constrain me, and the world is going to be whatever I can make it.*

The biblical story of creation sings a different song. When we join its chorus, it shapes our moral imagination quite differently. If we take the song of Genesis and let it shape our moral imagination, we can envision that we are not self-made beings, nor is this world a project of our own design. Living well is the moral vision of the doctrine of creation. Genesis 1–2 paints a vivid picture of the good life. It is the life in which the work of love is free to flourish. God is free to love the humans, the humans are free to return that love to God, and in so doing, they are also free to extend the work of love to the rest of the created order and to one another. Genesis 1–2 is the ballad of humans who are invited into the dynamics of the world God has created and charged with caring for that creation *within the good order God has established.*

At this point, we must acknowledge that sentences like the one I've just written have too often been used by humans to take control of the world around them. The concept of order has been abused, and we should do everything we can to avoid perpetuating that abuse. As a moral concept, order has been an alluring lever for those who would attempt to bend creation toward their desires in ways that suck the life out of others around them. For example,

Christians across the past several centuries have made appeals to "the created order" to justify the enslavement of people groups because those groups were supposed to be *ordered* toward (created for) compulsory service.[8] More recently, those who have supported social policies of racial segregation—such as South Africa's apartheid regime or the Jim Crow laws of the American South—made overt appeals to Genesis and the notion of separation found therein. Similar arguments have been employed to make the case that women are to be socially and physically subordinate as the natural order of God's creation.[9] We are pressed to reject these arguments, and any like them, because these approaches are not only another version of ordering creation as if we were the Creator, but they also do it in a way that ignores the divine intent for the work of love to go on freely. In opting for some version of order that subjects others in unloving ways, we demonstrate that we have missed one of the most significant aspects of what Christians affirm when we repeat to one another, "In the beginning, God created the heavens and the earth."

Taking the creation narrative as a whole reminds us that *the ordering work of God we see narrated in the opening chapters of Genesis serves to open the possibility of human freedom*, rather than closing it off. Further, the order God

THE WORK OF LOVE IN THE CREATED ORDER

---

8. John Wesley rejected arguments for institutional slavery that depended on African people being created for this purpose. See Wesley, "Thoughts upon Slavery," *Works*, 11:59–79.

9. Any notion that women are to be subordinate to men comes as a result of the fall, and is not the original intent for human beings. Additionally, I have noted already that the word used in Genesis 2 to describe the newly created human is *adam* ("dirtling"), rather than *ish* ("man"). The Hebrew words for "man" and "woman" come into play only after the *adam* has been divided in two. Though most English translations obscure it, the text does not suggest that a man was created first and a woman later. Rather, there was one human flesh that was divided into male and female when no animals were found to be suitable helpers. "Bone of my bones and flesh of my flesh" (Gen. 2:23) signals mutuality and equality rather than subordination.

establishes in the garden has to do with what the human beings are authorized to do so that the work of love might flourish, rather than the way love is thwarted by structures of subordination and domination. Wesley's reminder is helpful here: the way God has ordered creation is for *all* of creation's mutual benefit. We could say it this way: Do we see places in the world today that tend to close off the work of love, rather than open it up? Systems, structures, attitudes, and policies that act as a stepladder to effectively harvest forbidden fruit are most likely violations of the good order of creation, and we should name them as such. At the end of that harvest, we may end up with a basket full of fruit that will only lead to death.

As created beings who were breathed to life in the garden, we are made to extend the work of love that was first extended to us by God toward one another, to God, and toward the rest of the creation. Systems of oppression, sexism, racism, poverty, and the like are invasive weeds in creation's garden, and the calling of the creatures made in God's image is to join God's work of bringing chaos to order so that love can flourish. Subduing creation in a way that makes me the master of creation is not a truthful way to live as a created being. Rather, we joyfully and lovingly discover our place in this world as we ascertain what kind of beings we are in relationship to the God who lovingly creates and to the rest of creation we are called to love. The doctrine of creation affirms that God ordered creation in a way that maximizes the work of love toward neighbor and the rest of the created order.

Freedom for the Work of Love and the Vision of the Good Life

"You are free to eat from any tree in the garden," God says to the first human, according to Genesis 2. "But you must not eat from the tree of the knowledge of good and evil, for when you eat from it, you will certainly die" (Gen. 2:16b–17). Though this passage ranks among the most well known in Scripture, the moral importance often eludes us—especially that the freedom of creation to participate in love depends on the limits that are part of creation's order. Did you notice that, in this passage, God leads with freedom and that the freedom God gives then requires some limits? In the same way God had to limit the water from the land so that life could flourish in the sea and on the land, God works for human freedom by establishing us as morally reliant beings.

At first glance, it may seem odd or conflicted to associate freedom with limits. After all, isn't freedom directly opposed to limits? It's important for us to make a distinction between the freedom we find here in Genesis and something like the notion of liberty. Sharing a common root with the terms "liberated" and "liberal," *liberty* signals the absence of external constraints. A life of liberty is a life that has been able to break away from or shrug off any and all claims that anyone or anything would seek to make upon us from the outside. *Freedom,* on the other hand, seeks to enable a person for a task or purpose, often without dismantling all the external claims.

One example of freedom is the young woman who wakes up before the sun rises, puts on a pair of running shoes, and sets out for a planned jog of twenty miles. She has nothing on her calendar for the day, and she has the day off work. In essence, there are no external constraints being levied against her; she is at *liberty* to run twenty miles. We know, though, that just because she has the *liberty* to run such a long distance does not make her *free* to complete the course. Her freedom to run also has to do with the claim that has been made on her, morning after morning, when she has tied on the same pair of shoes and set out for a jog. While she was at liberty to stay in her warm bed on all those mornings, that liberty alone did not produce the freedom that she now has to run twenty miles.

Something similar is taking place in Genesis 2. "You are free," God says. Yet that freedom is produced by a corresponding limit: do not eat from *that* tree. The limit given helps produce freedom. The question of why God would place a tree in the garden that humanity should not eat from is not a question the text wants to answer. What we can find there is the formation of a moral relationship between God and creation that promotes creation's freedom, precisely as it comes to live within its contingency in the order God has established. *Humans are made to be free*, we can hear ringing through the text, *and that freedom springs from living within the good order God has established.* Living as if we are self-governed beings is not only untruthful but also cuts against our freedom.

Without limits, freedom suffers. Without acknowledging our moral contingency, we are not free to be God's creatures and participate fully in the goodness of God's creation. Pursuing any number of moral trajectories of our own setting means we close ourselves off to the good order God has established for love to flourish most freely. "In the absence of definitive limits," Brent Waters reminds us, "the resulting frenetic activity is enslaving, for one is captive to feeding the insatiable appetite of the self-made self."[10]

Gladly, the work of Christian ethics is done in the soil of a garden that humans did not plant but that allows us the freedom to live and love as God's contingent creatures. The moment we attempt to remake the garden, to shake ourselves away from being contingent creatures, is the moment when our work shifts from joining God's creative work and turns toward the service of the self. Or, to follow

---

10. Brent Waters, *This Mortal Flesh: Incarnation and Bioethics* (Grand Rapids: Brazos Press, 2009), 39.

the narrative of Genesis, it is to move from working the garden God has given us to building a tower to make a great name for ourselves (see Gen. 11:1–4). Freedom and contingency are not opposed to one another. Our freedom grows out of our dependence on God's gift of life-giving breath that fills our lungs and speaks order into chaos.

It is entirely likely that Genesis 3, guided by the inspiration of God's Holy Spirit, is making a theological comment about the results of the human impulse to chart a moral course according to self-serving desires, rather than delighting in the freedom to love one another well. This narrative offers a clear reminder that we will often come face to face with the temptation to throw off our contingency and take the knowledge of good and evil into our own hands.[11] "God knows good and evil, and human beings attain that godlike knowledge upon eating of the tree, though it is a knowledge with which they cannot live very well."[12]

As the story turns from the goodness of creation to taking an account of its fallenness, free relationships are barricaded and obstructed. The humans hide themselves from God and from each other, sensing a sudden need to clothe themselves, hiding their bodies from view. The relationship between the humans and the rest of the created order is strained as well, so that the ground fights back against the human work of calling it to flourish (3:17–19). The animals, too, are one more step removed from being suitable helpers (vv. 14–15).

We may be tempted to simply accept the limits of living within a fallen creation. "This is simply the way the world is," we might say fatalistically, and go on our way of

---

11. The phrase "good and evil" in this text implies a choice. It is not so much that it bestows absolute knowledge of good but that this knowledge allows us to know the difference between good and evil.

12. Terrence Fretheim, *New Interpreter's Bible* (Nashville: Abingdon Press, 1994), 1:350–51.

attempting to muddle through the best we can. The more excellent way, however, gives us a different moral vision. One of the Wesleyan convictions regarding fallenness is that it is no match for the grace God continues to pour out upon a creation that groans for redemption. The same Spirit that was breathing life into the humans in the garden continues to enliven humans for the work of love. The same Spirit that was working in creation is working in new creation. We are created-in-love beings who have been made to love freely, and God's work is restoring our capacity to do just that.

Our freedom allows us to engage the world, working against the disordered effects of sin, oppression, and injustice. We work with our aim in mind and toward the mutual blessing of the rest of creation, all for God's glory. By grace, we work against the thorns that grow up out of a fallen ground, choking out the avenues for love. Doing this work means love will flourish. The moment we reach for the fruit of self-sufficiency or moral authority, as tempting as it may be, is the moment we close off the dynamic of goodness that we met in the garden.

SEVEN

The Work of Jesus Christ

The work of Christian ethics derives from and expresses the work of Jesus Christ. The question in front of us now is the nature of that connection and what it means for the way Christian ethics are worked. As we explore the characteristic contributions that the Wesleyan tradition makes to Christian ethics, we should ask about what Wesleyans say about Jesus and his work. How might that shape the moral vision that guides the work of Christian ethics?

Wesley's approach to Christology—the study of the nature and work of Jesus Christ—was practical. "His focal christological concern was with the *work* of Christ."[1] When Wesley talked and taught about Jesus, it was usually for the sake of how God is *working* and how that might transform and redeem the kinds of work *we* do. When addressing that work, Wesley treated the Christian tradition as a deep well, and drew from it often. He was a product of and was responding to the explosion of theological development associated with the Reformation that tended to place a lot

---

1. Randy L. Maddox, *Responsible Grace: John Wesley's Practical Theology* (Nashville: Kingswood Books, 1994), 95. For those interested in the complexities of Wesley's Christology, including how he may have tended toward some extremes, I recommend John Deschner, *Wesley's Christology: An Interpretation* (Wilmore, KY: Francis Asbury Press, 1988); Maddox, *Responsible Grace*; and Kenneth J. Collins, *A Faithful Witness: John Wesley's Homiletical Theology* (Wilmore, KY: Wesley Heritage Press, 1993). Richard Riss has helpfully distilled the contours of that conversation into one article: "John Wesley's Christology in Recent Literature," *Wesleyan Theological Journal*, vol. 45 (2010).

of emphasis on the *legal* aspects of Christ's work. Though the work of their founders was more nuanced, a popular outworking of the Reformers' theology emphasized Christ's work as "covering up" the guilt of our sin.

Interestingly, Wesley drew together the legal themes of the Reformation and the themes of the Eastern stream of Christianity, which has historically seen the work of Christ as offering healing and transformation. For Wesley, Christ's work did cover up our guilt, but it also opened a dynamic, ongoing reality of redemption in which the infectious reality of sin was healed. Moral transformation is one of the outcomes of this redemption. It isn't so much that the Wesleyan tradition has offered novel discoveries in Christology as that it is marked by the healing aspects of Christ's work that it highlights. Those highlights shape the kind of moral vision through which Wesleyans see their work, and shape the way we understand our connection to the work of Jesus. We'll lift out some of those highlights in this chapter and ask how they offer us a more excellent way of doing the work of Christian ethics.

The Way (of the Cross), the Truth (Crucified), and the (Resurrected) Life

In the history of ethics, philosophers have often said there is a strong link between truth and goodness. If something was good, they said, it was also true. Often, they developed ethics that said life was good when it corresponded with truth. For example, the ancient Greek philosopher Plato argued that there were intangible and eternal truths called Forms, or Ideas. Ethics was the art of lining up one's actions with those eternal truths. And action would be *good* only insofar as it reflected what was *true*.

While I have reservations about simply adopting Plato's method into the work of Christian ethics, the incarnation of Jesus stands as an enduring reminder that truth and goodness are united in him. His life was good precisely because his life was true to God. The confession that God became flesh in Jesus is a proclamation that God was pleased to intermingle with the fallen realities of the world. It is a staggering confession because Jesus was especially pleased to dwell with those who had been pressed down and cast out from the vision of the good life in his day. The culture-challenging reality is that if *Jesus* was pleased to dwell there, with them, in that way, it was a revelation of *God's* intention to dwell there, with them, in that way. The incarnation of Jesus came as a challenge to most notions of goodness the world had seen.

Affirming that Jesus was God in the flesh also meant that what we saw him do was *good* because it was also *true* to who God is. Far from Plato's vision of true goodness living at a distance from the everyday realities of human life, the Christian affirmation of incarnation is the good news that goodness has come to stand in the place where goodness has been withheld or blocked by the sinful actions of humans. Ethics is especially Christian when it works out of the reality that God became flesh, walking and working with the poor and oppressed. If Christian theology is the attempt to speak carefully and truthfully in response to the Word that has been spoken to us, then Christian ethics is the thoughtful attempt to live truthfully in response to the Word that was spoken to us in the incarnation of Jesus. Theology and ethics cannot be divided because truth and goodness are united in Jesus.

John's Gospel gives us a fascinating exchange that is rife with moral implication. Thomas asks Jesus a question: "Lord, we don't know where you are going, so how can we know the way?" Jesus responds, "I am the way and the truth and the life" (John 14:5, 6). In this phrase, we can see that all three—way, truth, life—are united in Jesus. As the *way*, he is *true*, and he is *life*. In part, this means we can't hold life apart from truth or way. To walk a way that is true is also what it looks like to be truly *alive*. When our way is patterned in truth, we spring to full, expressive, and vibrant life.

In some significant ways, Thomas reflects a dynamic we often encounter in ethics today. When he comes to Jesus in John 14, he is asking a relatively simple question: "How can we know the way?" I suspect many of us approach ethics in a similar way. We aren't looking to rethink everything. Our request is relatively simple: *Tell me the way. What do I do?* It doesn't need to be complicated. It only needs to point us to "do the right thing."

In his distinctive way, though, Jesus takes an approach that might expose us to a glimpse of goodness and instead leads us into the depths of goodness, challenging as that may be. Notice that Jesus doesn't give Thomas a clear-cut set of directions. He doesn't tell Thomas which rules to follow or which moral principles will make him a "good person." He does, however, state that he *is* the way, the truth, and the life. If we are left wondering what that looks like, I suspect John 20 provides an answer that plunges us into the depths of truth and goodness. In that chapter, which happens to contain the next time Thomas shows up in John's Gospel, Jesus stands before the disciples in his resurrected body and issues an invitation: "Reach out your hand and put it into my side" (v. 27). There, in that locked room, the disciples encounter the unity of way, truth, and life. The Way is the way of the cross, the Truth has been crucified, and the Life is resurrection. In his incarnated, crucified, resurrected body, Jesus unites the way, the truth, and the life—and he invites us into that kind of life. The way, the truth, and the life cannot be held apart from the realities of incarnation, crucifixion, and resurrection. An ethics in the way of Jesus testifies to a true way that makes us alive in the pattern of Christ's life. That life—the true life—is lived in the way of drawing near, being faithful to the point of death, and entrusting the Father with whatever kind of resurrected future results.

We know our actions are true when the way of our life is true to Jesus, who entrusted every aspect of his being to the Father in the power of the Spirit. Christian ethics is far more than a moral calculator designed to show us right from wrong. Christian ethics is the art of discerning whether the way of our lives is *true*. If our way is true, there is life. Jesus is the Way, the Truth, and the Life.

The capacity to come to life in the pattern of Jesus is a gift of God. It moves beyond simply asking what Jesus would do and attempting to imitate it. It plunges us into what Jesus is currently doing—inviting us into the way that is true and that gives us life. These are no abstract principles we are talking about. These are flesh-and-blood realities. Jesus's *way* puts him at odds with the powers and principalities around him. The *truth* exposes those powers for what they are, and they fight back. The *life* Jesus is given is true, resurrected life that comes with the scars of his crucifixion. While we might be able to get by with Christian ethics being a kind of debate, disconnected from the work of life, the more excellent way is the truth of a life, given in faithfulness to the Father in the power of the Spirit. It is a true life that probably won't prevent us from taking on scars, but it is the way of the One who lived a truly human life, and calls us to life in his pattern. It is the way of working in the world that places the outcome of our life's work into the care of the Father, entrusting that any truth in our work will be seen in resurrection.

The Work of Atonement

Stemming from the conviction that humans have been alienated from God, atonement theology confesses that Jesus has made a way for God and humanity to relate well. Across the centuries of Christian history, the worldwide church has never come to a single view of what was happening in Jesus's work that made for atonement. Some tend to place the emphasis on the moral example Jesus offered in his death; others find power in the way Jesus restores God's due honor in spite of a rebellious creation; still others see the atonement as a moral victory over evil.

The Wesleyan view of the atonement is that it is primarily about God's gracious and loving work in Christ to reestablish the relationship between God and creation so humans can reflect the image of God. All three of the atonement theories I just mentioned are present in this vision to some degree. But for Wesleyans, the atonement is not about an enraged God seeking revenge against rebellious humans who have done wrong. This is a loving God seeking reconciliation at all costs so that humans can thrive—imagine a loving parent pursuing, seeking, and welcoming home a wayward child. "The subject of the atonement," Deschner reminds us, of Wesley's theology, "is the God-man, seen from the perspective of his divine nature but provided with a human nature as a necessary instrument for his atoning work, which consists primarily in his death, not so much *as* man, as *for* man."[2] Wesley's understanding of the atonement was not humans needing to be punished so much as a uniquely divine and human Person opening the way for humans to be liberated for moral freedom.

The ethical implications here can't be overstated. The degree to which we consider Jesus's work on the cross to be about taking the punishment that a morally violated God must dole out is the degree to which our moral vision will likely be guided by fearful subservience or the zealous attempt to correct the ethical violations of both ourselves and those around us. If the atonement is primarily about appeasing a God of wrath, Christian ethics will most likely

---

2. Deschner, *Wesley's Christology*, 167, emphasis added.

take the shape of figuring out what we must do to soothe God's anger, and proceed from that point. Armed with the moral knowledge that God's wrath is coming for the ultimately disobedient, Christians may turn toward their neighbors in hopes of correcting noncompliant behavior. The moral vision becomes one of addressing ethical violations and calling for—even demanding—their correction.

If, however, the atonement is a movement on God's part to reestablish the relationship that graciously offers humans the essence of new creation, our moral vision has the capacity to shift our focus toward working Christian ethics in response to God's redemptive work. Now, obedience becomes a joyful response to the love we experience in God's gracious work. Obedience is a moral byproduct of becoming a new creation. We are invited into freedom, rather than compliant by demand. Our moral posture toward our neighbors can then become one of proclamation rather than condemnation. If what we saw on the cross was a demonstration of divine love *par excellence*, it's only natural for us to speak this good news. We turn toward our neighbors to proclaim that abundant life has been opened to us by a God who became flesh in order that we might be made new. "If we will respond to this pardoning love of God and allow God's presence deeper access to our lives, then we will be liberated from our captivity to sin, and the process of our transformation into the fullness that God has always intended for us can begin."[3]

The Work of Recapitulation

When Paul writes to the Christians in Corinth about "the last Adam," he offers a thread that has since been woven through the historical tapestry of Christian faith (1 Cor. 15:45). In Christ's work, he sees a reversal of the

3. Maddox, *Responsible Grace*, 109.

death that has grasped at all humans since Adam. If all of humanity was held under the influence of what went wrong when the first humans decided to take things into their own hands and diminish the image of God that was the very essence of their life, then the work of Jesus breaks that hold. Paul proclaims that the work of Jesus has ruptured the vessel of degradation that we all live in. "For as in Adam all die, so in Christ all will be made alive" (15:22).

To the church in Ephesus, Paul writes that we have been chosen "in him" for adoption (Eph. 1:3–10). Swept up in the redemptive operation of divine grace, we are the beneficiaries of our fallen humanity being taken up in Christ's perfected humanity. Being adopted in Christ and made alive is responsively joining the dynamic of Father, Son, and Holy Spirit that has been bringing things to life from the dawn of creation. When the Father spoke the Word in the power of the Spirit, primordial chaos became the flourishing order of good creation. The same is true of humans in a moral sense, according to Wesley's theology. Apart from the ordering Word that became flesh in Jesus, we live in a state of chaos. The same creative Word the Father spoke then is spoken to us now, and in the life-giving power of the Spirit, chaos gives way to flourishing. Morally, slavery gives way to freedom. "The purpose of Christ's coming," Randy Maddox says of Wesley's theology, "is to reclaim human life, free us from slavery, and restore our participation in God. Christ reclaims human life by joining the divine nature with our human nature and 'recapitulating' all the states of human life (including death.)"[4]

Linguists tell us that the term "recapitulation" has declined in use over the past two hundred years, so its implications may be lost on us. During the nineteenth century, it was a musical term. In a sonata, for example, a composer

---

4. Maddox, *Responsible Grace*, 97.

would state a musical theme, like a melody. That theme would then be developed and later recapitulated when the composer brought the theme back to the listener's ears. "Oh, I remember that song!" we might say when we hear a long-forgotten melody from our childhood. Similarly, Christ *recapitulates* humanity. "Oh, I remember those creatures!" we could say when we see Jesus, who picks up the theme of humanity that was composed in the garden but began to decompose under the effects of sin. As the "second Adam," he is everything humanity was meant to be, and he therefore does everything humanity was meant to do.

Sin, of course, is not simply doing a bad thing or violating some kind of social code. Sin is the word we've given to the dense and complex web of forces that move us from life to death. It is the impulse to turn away from the source of life, and it is the self-destructive drive to do what we know kills us. Paul writes in a way that suggests he is not joking: "For the wages of sin is death, but the gift of God is eternal life in Christ Jesus our Lord" (Rom. 6:23). Paul's message is one of recapitulation. Life is *in* Christ Jesus, who has taken up human nature in an act of recapitulation and restored the potential of life to humans. In carrying forth the theme of humanity, Jesus allows us to sing along with the melody of a life lived in freedom and in reconciled relationship with God and our neighbors. The work he does in recapitulation opens the way for us to do true moral work in the world.

In this way, Jesus is far more than a moral example. Jesus is the *way* of moral life. In him, human beings are alive and free to be what God intended. The Wesleyan approach to Christian ethics can then make this profound claim: morality isn't just about *doing* the right thing but about being made alive in Christ Jesus. While some approaches to Christian ethics involve a host of strategies to determine right and wrong and striving for the former, the Wesleyan approach has a lot more to do with participating in God's redemptive work and coming to life as a result. "When you were slaves to sin, you were free from the control of righteousness" (Rom. 6:20). The problem was that this was the kind of freedom our bodies experience when we are "free" from oxygen—it leads to death. "You have been set free from sin and have become slaves to righteousness . . . so now offer yourselves as slaves to righteousness leading to holiness" (Rom. 6:18, 19c).

Sometimes Christian ethics is seen as the ability to calculate the difference between the right and wrong and trying to avoid the wrong. Perhaps that approach wouldn't be an entire loss. There is a more excellent way, though, and that is understanding the moral life as a life freed to be alive. That is a way made possible through Christ's recapitulation of human life. The life of Jesus is the fullest expression of human life. It is true and complete humanity recapitulated, opening to us the possibility of a true and complete human life. "When we look at Jesus, we know what it means to be truly human because he shows us what a human life looks like when it is lived in perfect relationship with the Father by the power of the Holy Spirit," Beth Felker Jones helps us see. "Because he shows us what *true* humanity looks like, Jesus Christ alone enables us to practice being human."[5]

---

5. Beth Felker Jones, *Practicing Christian Doctrine: An Introduction to Thinking and Living Theologically* (Grand Rapids: Baker Academic, 2014), 98–99.

EIGHT

The Work of Being Human

It may seem strange to find a chapter on being human in a book on Christian ethics, but the Wesleyan tradition's take on humanity is too rich a resource to ignore. As we begin, it would be helpful to consider the story of humanity that has shaped our moral imagination. Take a moment and ask yourself, *What do I think it means to be human? What makes me human?* The way you answer those questions will probably reveal the story that has been passed on to you about humanity. Though it may have happened ever so silently, messages about what it means to be human have likely shaped the way we imagine the shape of our moral life.

The story in Genesis of what it means to be human differs from the one I suspect many of us have inherited. In our version of the story, our humanity is a moral problem. It may even be *the* problem—the villainous but inescapable reality that holds us back from being truly good. Carried to us on the backs of phrases like, "I'm only human!" and "the sins of the flesh," this story suggests a subtle but important message: our humanity is a problem for our morality. Approaching our humanity in this way closes off a world of moral possibility. It reduces ethics to little more than a quest to avoid doing wrong things or a set of rules to be followed unimaginatively. The more excellent way is a moral vision of humanity that envisions what it means to be human in terms of God's life-giving love.

For thousands of years, ethicists have inquired about what *kind* of beings humans are, arguing that the kind of beings we are gives us a pathway to morality. Many have claimed that humans ought not be held to a moral standard that exceeds what they naturally are, so the *kind* of being a human is should shape the type of moral work they do.[1] We don't expect a baseball glove to do the work of a kitchen whisk because of the *kind* of tool it is. The *kind* of being a human is, then, shapes our expectations for the work that is expected of us. For Christians, the work of ethics is not about somehow transcending or escaping our humanity to do work that is superhuman, but it is about doing good work as the creatures God created us to be.

What Are Human Beings That You Care for Them?[2]

The exploration of what humans are usually takes place in a conversation called "theological anthropology," or the study of what it means to be human in relation to God. Anthropologists study the formation of human societies and human behavior, but *theological* anthropologists ask about what kinds of creatures we are as those created in God's image.[3] Theological anthropology helps us face

---

1. David Hume and Adam Smith are prominent examples of this kind of thinking. Hume questioned how we might prescribe some kind of moral *ought* based on what *is*. When we see the way something *is*, he reasoned, why would we say that it *ought* to be different? Smith adopted a similar principle when it came to economic exchange. Though we may have some knowledge of persons living on the other side of the world, he said, our nature as local beings, situated in a particular place, means we are morally responsible mainly to those who are closest to us. See Hume's *A Treatise of Human Nature* and Smith's *The Wealth of Nations*.

2. Paraphrase of Psalm 8:4.

3. The Greek word *anthropos* is often translated as "human," and *theos* in Greek is the term for God. Thus, *theological anthropology* is more than studying how humans relate to one another but also includes how humans relate to God. I've also heard people object to using the term "creatures" to refer to humans

down some confusion that has probably shaped our moral vision. For decades, many of us have taken in a version of the salvation story that begins with our sinfulness. The "Romans Road," a distillation of the gospel message that has been popular among evangelicals, begins by pointing to humanity's sin problem. While Wesleyans have no argument with the reality that "all have sinned and fall short of the glory of God" (Rom. 3:23), we should be careful not to equate the *beginning* of the story with human sin. The beginning of the story is that humans have been lovingly created in God's image. Popularly, beginning with human sin has clouded our understanding of what kind of creatures we are, and the version of the story many of us have inherited may be whispering to us that sin is what defines us as creatures.

The anthropological claim that humans are created in the image of God issues a hope-filled challenge to notions of humanity that suggest sin defines us as creatures. Since we will never be rid of the sin problem, the thinking goes, our best hope for morality is to ask for God's help managing the sin. If sin is what defines humans, the moral possibilities live within the boundaries of sin. We work out an ethics as best we can with the aid of grace but in the understanding that our ethics cannot expect us to break free from sin entirely.

What might happen to our work if humans were not defined primarily according to the sin that entangles us? What kind of work might we be capable of imagining? What kind of moral imagination might be opened up to us if we

---

because they think it makes humans too animalistic. At its root, though, "creatures" is like "create"—simply pointing to humans as created beings. Finally, if the temptation to object to the term "creatures" is based in the notion that it makes humans too much like animals, consider that even the term "animal" shares a root with "animate," signaling a created being that is animated by God's very breath. In this way, we can affirm that we humans are creatures and—like the other species with which we share the earth—are animated (brought to life) by God.

understand ourselves primarily in terms of our relationship to God? Such is the Wesleyan vision of the Christian faith tradition, and the one that enlivens our imagination here. While acknowledging that humans were indeed universally affected by sin, John Wesley also refused to allow sin to define what *kind* of creatures human beings are. Sin is not what makes us human. Sin enslaves us to the detriment of our humanity. Wesley's great hope was that God's grace is more powerful than the life-sucking effects of sin upon all humans. Through an ongoing and ever-deepening relationship with God, human beings become more fully alive as we open ourselves to the transformation God effects through grace. In Wesley's language, "the great end of religion is to renew our hearts in the image of God."[4] For him, the kind of creatures we humans are is found in the way we are *alive* in God's image, reflecting the divine image. "The primary relation constituting the *imago Dei*," H. Ray Dunning has written, "is humanity's relation to God."[5]

Many Christians have found the metaphor of a mirror to be helpful in understanding the image of God. According to the metaphor we are like mirrors, made to reflect the divine image to the world around us. Sin is like dirt on the mirror—it clouds and distorts the image of God that should be seen in us. I like this metaphor for a couple of reasons. First, it signals that the image of God is not something humans possess innately, the way Augustine thought of sin as being encoded into human nature. "A mirror does not possess the image it reflects," Theodore Runyon helpfully articulates.[6] This reality beckons toward a second point: the image of God is a *relational* dynamic. The more closely

---

4. Wesley, "Original Sin," *Works*, 6:64.

5. H. Ray Dunning, *Reflecting the Divine Image: Christian Ethics in Wesleyan Perspective* (Eugene, OR: Wipf and Stock, 2003), 45.

6. Theodore Runyon, "The New Creation: A Wesleyan Distinctive," *Wesleyan Theological Journal*, vol. 31, no. 2 (Fall 1996), 8.

humans relate to God, the more the image of God is reflected in our lives. Rather than being hard-wired into the human genome as if to physically resemble God, or being found in the human capacity for rational thought as some have suggested, the image of God is *God's* image reflected by those who have been transformed by grace to resemble God more and more.

Made in the Image of God

The moral stakes are too high to leave the phrase "the image of God" unexplored. Historically, appeals to the image of God have been weaponized by those who wish God to be made in their own image, to the violent and appalling detriment of those who may not fit the predetermined image. The horrifying efforts of the Nazi regime were not only an example of the image of God being manipulated into acts of violence but were also a theological error that birthed a moral calamity. At once, the architects of the Final Solution determined that some characteristics of Jews were to be erased from the human gene pool and that those with disabilities and abnormalities of various sorts were to be seen as less than human. When we locate the image of God in physical characteristics, or in the capacity for rationality, we are only a short step away from the possibility of claiming that those who differ physically from the majority or do not possess the same capacities for rationality as others are not in the image of God.

One of the promising aspects of establishing the image of God in relational terms is that it neither reduces the image to a set of physical manifestations nor excludes those with reduced rational capacity from being seen as in God's image.[7] Consider the earnest prayers of a young child, for

---

7. For an insightful analysis of the way physical characteristics have been employed in racialized ways, see Brian Bantum, *The Death of Race: Building a New*

example. While it would not be difficult to acknowledge that the child may not have the same capacity for rationally understanding what she is doing by praying, we would be hard-pressed to say the child is somehow a lesser reflection of God's image. Her childlike faith may in fact be *more* of a reflection of the divine than those who have devoted their adult lives to the study of prayer. Taking this view of the human being to heart means the capacity to reflect the image of God is not found in one's physical characteristics, one's capacity for rational thought, or in one's national identity or place of birth. Complementing the Wesleyan view of theological anthropology is its understanding of God's grace as *prevenient,* meaning it extends to all creation, even before we are aware of its influence. This is the grace that gifts any person to be capable of responding to God's movement and to have the image of God become more fully realized. The moral point here is that, by virtue of God's grace, *all humans have the capacity to reflect the image of God.*

The Wesleyan view of grace compels us to affirm that those who have been afflicted by the dehumanizing evils of addiction, systemic poverty, violence, oppression, or racism are sustained by God's grace. By virtue of God relating to people everywhere through the operation of prevenient grace, every person reflects the image of God. If God's outreaching, gracious activity continuously extends to all humans, our moral vision of those humans is to see them as beings "capable of God," to use Wesley's phrase.[8] Christian ethics in the Wesleyan tradition begins here when it comes to our relationship with our fellow humans. It follows in

---

Christianity in a Racial World (Minneapolis: Fortress Press, 2016).

8. Wesley, "The General Deliverance," *Works,* 6:241–52. In this sermon, Wesley writes that the first human "was a creature capable of God; capable of knowing, loving, and obeying his Creator." The relational dynamic is unmistakable: the image of God is not a capacity humans possess apart from God but is one that flourishes the more one lives in reconciled relationship to God.

We should be careful not to equate the beginning of the story with human sin. The beginning of the story is that humans have been lovingly created in God's image.

concrete action that is meant to enable our neighbors to more fully reflect God's image, to extend to those around us the good news of reconciliation, rather than viewing them "from a worldly point of view" (2 Cor. 5:16–20). While mere tolerance of others isn't a moral evil, it comes up short of the more excellent way, which includes reconciliation in the love of Christ. We work against the grain of God's grace if we look at another human and act as if God's image cannot be reflected through them. It is to our common detriment if we miss out on catching a glimpse of the beauty of the divine image reflected to us through someone because they differ from us.

Going a step further, this view of grace calls us to celebrate the gift God has given to us in our neighbors. In approaching another person, consider their creation as a being capable of reflecting the divine image. Before they are a coworker, employee, spouse, service worker, supervisor, or stranger on the street, they are a being who has been created to reflect the divine image. To mistreat them is to turn a blind eye to the image of the divine and close off the image of a loving God from being reflected to them from us. As H. Ray Dunning has written, "If we are truly reflecting the divine image in interpersonal relations, we can never turn other persons into things to be used for our own self-centered ends. We cannot treat them as an 'it.'"[9]

The Image of the Invisible God

The fullest expression of the image of God in the Christian faith, of course, is Jesus Christ, "the image of the invisible God" (Col. 1:15). But what is it about Jesus that makes this the case? It is that Jesus is in complete communion with the Father through the Spirit. Jesus is fully and completely related to God by virtue of his perfect commu-

---

9. Dunning, *Reflecting the Divine Image*, 93.

nion with God as a Person of the Trinity. If it is his perfect communion within the Trinity that makes Jesus fully divine, that is also what makes Jesus fully human! Jesus is fully human precisely because his life is an unreserved openness to the Father through the Spirit.

The bold and vibrant optimism of the Wesleyan tradition proclaims that the perfect communion of relationship that makes Jesus fully alive as a human also opens to us and invites us in! God's life of love opens to all humanity, graciously inviting them to be made capable of reflecting God to the world around them. At God's gracious and hospitable invitation, we may "participate in the divine nature," not becoming divine, but becoming fully human because we reflect the divine (2 Pet. 1:4). In this regard, the more we are made to be like Christ, the more fully human we become. *Christlikeness*, then, is not a moral goal toward which humans are meant to strive under our own power. Rather, it is a gift given to us by a God whose life is open to us, welcoming us into a transformational relationship of love.

The moral vision of what I'm suggesting now begins to arrive in view. The approach to ethics in the Wesleyan tradition isn't reasoning our way toward an action, but it is the responsive opening of ourselves to a fuller relationship with God. Ethics in the Wesleyan tradition is renewal of the heart that is the renewal of the image of God, which is also the holy life, which is also the moral life. In becoming more fully human, we are given the gift of lives that are aligned to the way God is making all things new!

The Work of Being Human

Let's return briefly to the claim that the shape of the moral life is a more excellent way. When Wesley used this phrase as the title of one of his sermons, he was pointing to a life transformed by love. There are generally two kinds of Christians, he asserts. There are those who are living adequate and faithful lives, who tend to live "void of offence . . . being in most things like their neighbours."[10] These are the folks who have become accustomed to avoiding vice as well-adjusted members of society. They are those who don't cheat their neighbors in business dealings, who don't break the law, and who rarely would let a disparaging word about an acquaintance fall from their lips.

The life Wesley goes on to describe as the more excellent way isn't satisfied with simply avoiding bad things and leading an ethically adequate existence. It is the life that opts to "aspire after the heights and depths of holiness—after the *entire image of God*."[11] It's the life that isn't satisfied with simply not cheating our neighbors or refraining from gossip, but a life devoted to being utterly and completely transformed, such that the *desire* for things like cheating and gossip are swallowed up by the transforming grace that renews us in the image of God. It is an "above and beyond" moral life that is a gift from God, the life of one who has come to "'know all that love of God which passeth knowledge, and to be filled with all the fullness of God.'"[12] The more excellent way is not simply a moderately good life but a life renewed by God into something "very good." The moral impulse of this theological vision is that, as we humans become more aligned with God's new creation, we also become more fully alive! Morality isn't something added to our humanity; it is the result of a human becoming more fully alive in the likeness of Jesus. Our humanity is not a barrier to moral goodness but an invitation to joyfully respond to God's grace.

There is a kind of moral virtue in this vision of humanity. It's found in the way we respond to the grace being

10. Wesley, "The More Excellent Way," 7:28.
11. Wesley, "The More Excellent Way," 7:28, emphasis added.
12. Wesley, "The More Excellent Way, 7:28.

offered to us and the way we take up the means of that grace. The work of being human begins long before we are faced with a moral dilemma. It is the work God does in transforming our hearts to long for the more excellent way. It is the work that considers how our moral decisions affect other humans, all of whom have the potential to reflect the image of God. This is hopeful work too—precisely because Christian ethics is not simply about managing our sinful impulses or striving to avoid doing bad things. It's a life of freedom that (re)creates humans to be what we were always intended to be: *orthokardia* beings in deep, life-giving relationship with God, and in loving relationship with one another. This is humanity reflecting the image of God. This is humanity that isn't simply interested in living a moderately good life but humanity that God has created, recreated, and declared to be very good.

NINE

The Work of the People
New Creation Ethics and the Life of the Church

By now, I hope we have seen that all of Christian ethics is concerned with the work of the people. In this chapter, though, we turn our attention to what it means to do the work of the people as the church. To treat the church as a voluntary association of individuals or a religious organization misses the moral point. We are not talking about an ethical support group designed to establish in us good morals. The church is a far more radical reality, a living entity of God's new creation. John Wesley's lifelong effort to bring a reforming vitality to the church demonstrates that the gathering of believers was more than a holding tank for folks who happened to agree with one another on matters of spirituality. In the church, something new is being born in the midst of old creation.

The early church, to borrow Richard Hays's description, was a group that "found its identity and vocation by recognizing its role within the cosmic drama of God's reconciliation of the world to himself."[1] The church is not a static community for those who are merely convinced that something is going to happen in the life to come but a living reality of what God is doing now. The church is

---

1. Hays, *The Moral Vision of the New Testament*, 19.

what happens when the Spirit of God breathes a bit of new creation life into a world that is groaning under the weight of its own pain. The way that church moves and lives and works is its ethics.

Of course, not every group that gets together and calls itself a church lives out these realities. Unfortunately, the crosses lifted high above certain buildings don't always reflect the lives being led by those who gather there weekly. This is why it's important to remember that the Wesleyan movement has been intent on reviving and renewing the church. It is the optimistic call to the church that there is a more excellent way than simply establishing some principles and digging deeply into our wills to try to follow them. If our view of the church is a community meant to produce more ethical, well-adjusted citizens, we have missed the radical call to holiness that is the life of the church. While there may not be anything overtly wrong with being kinder and nicer, the more excellent way calls the church to remember it is a holy people, given over to God's purposes of renewing our world by taking on the name and pattern of Jesus and living in the freedom of his way by the grace of God's Spirit with us. Often, this means our devotion to a God who is bringing about a new creation will put us at odds with the rhythms of old creation's status quo.

When we turn to consider the church, we must remember we aren't trying to preserve a moral vision that makes our lives manageable, consistent, or socially well adjusted. The church isn't so much an arena in which answers to moral issues are debated and solved as the living body that is walking out the way life is when Christ's tomb is empty. That's not to say the church doesn't do the work of moral discernment together. The point is that we are discerning *toward* something more than how to make all parties happy or how to achieve an outcome that fits our social context with a bit more relevance. We are discerning *toward* the new creation that God is giving. Our discernment is aligned to ask, "How might we act in a way that opens new creation in the midst of the old?"

Additionally, Christian ethics in the Wesleyan way isn't attempting to merely preserve whatever shred of order remains intact in the fallen world, as some approaches to Christian ethics suggest the church's moral purpose is. To do so would be to settle for far less than our own theology tells us is possible. The more excellent way is to lean into the reality that the church is what happens on the way to the world being made new. It is a group of people who do the work of new creation even before the project is finished. Wherever people are empowered by the Spirit to live in the reality of the good news that Christ's tomb is empty, and wherever they are gifted with a life together that resembles the new creation because of that news, there is the church.

The Work of the (New Creation) People

For as long as there has been something called "church," Christians have talked about the work they do together. "Liturgy" is the name we give to that work now. If that word conjures in your imagination a ritualistic pattern of religious ceremonies that are disconnected from real life, it may be an impediment to what that word expressed for most of the church's history. Literally meaning "the work of the people," liturgy is simply what people do when they gather together.

In light of God making the world new through Jesus, the earliest churches were asking, "What do we *do* now?" What they did in light of the empty tomb and how they came to determine what to do was their ethics. It was the work they rendered in a world that seemed to be falling apart around them but also a world where the reality of Christ's resurrection could not be ignored. It was the work that made them who they were. The work they did—and the work the church should continue to do—is the working out of Christ's resurrection through the power of the Spirit. The work of the people is *the body of Christ working in hope of the resurrection and the life to come.*

It is important to remember that the work the church is called to is holy work—set apart for God's purposes. This admonition comes with a confession: churches often find themselves doing work that is not hopeful or representative of Christ's body. Keeping the themes of Christ's body working in the hope of resurrection offers us a kind of discernment guide to consider what we are doing. Has our work abandoned the proclamation of the empty tomb? Has it become mundane, turned toward the mere effort of keeping a building open, maintaining a moral code, supporting a partisan political platform, or keeping an institution funded? Or has it turned toward the provocative, holy work of gesturing toward the empty tomb and asking, "Now what?"

The Body of Christ

The church is the living embodiment of the empty tomb's moral overflow. Echoing the evocative image of the creation of humanity, the church is a body that comes to life when the Spirit of God breathes into a collection of particles that couldn't do holy work on their own. Whether we are reading Luke's account of Pentecost in Acts 2 or that of Jesus breathing the Spirit onto his disciples in John 20, the Spirit breathes individual particles to life as a body, and that body begins to work. The church is an event of new creation—it's what *happens* when the Spirit breathes a body to life. Christian ethics is not so much about the individual persons trying to figure out what to do because they go to church as it is about discerning the work that this new body has been enlivened to do in the world, especially in light of the empty tomb.

In this way, the church doesn't *have* an ethics as much as it *is* an ethics. Borrowing the language of the earliest Christians, the gathering of believers in the world was simply the Way. It was a way of walking, a way of serving, a way of gathering, a way of sharing, a way of worshiping—a way of working. Breathed to life by the power of the Spirit, the church is the body whose life is doing the work of new creation. "For we were all baptized by one Spirit so as to form one body," Paul reminds the Corinthians (1 Cor. 12:13a). The way we gather, the way we use and arrange power dynamics, the way we forgive and listen, the way we handle conflict and hurt—all of this is our ethics, and the church is alive to be able to handle these things in a distinctly new creation way.

This body is not just any body, appealing to vague moral principles. It is the body *of Christ* (1 Cor. 12:27). All of its life takes its cues from a first-century carpenter whose work and way put him at odds with old creation. He didn't agitate for the sake of agitation, but he walked in step with new creation in a way that inevitably put him crossways with those who preferred the world as it was. If the church is to walk and live and work as the body of *Christ*, it cannot ignore the particular and discomforting way Jesus walked. To be the body of Christ, the church's walk must be in step with Jesus, even if we fall out of step with old creation realities, partisan political platforms, or business as usual. If we cannot join the way of Jesus, we have nothing to offer the world that is new.

Inevitably, this means the church should consider how it can't walk in step with old creation realities while being the body of Christ. Its mission isn't to seek out how to simply get along more kindly with the realities that have a vested interest in keeping old creation old. The church is what happens when the new creation inaugurated in Jesus Christ springs to life here and now by the power of the Spirit. As nice as that sounds, we must remember that it will put the church at odds with social, political, economic, and moral systems that can't see past old creation to the new thing God is doing in Jesus. The way of Jesus is distinct. It can't be boiled down to vague sets of values, and it doesn't fit hand-in-glove inside other systems. It will always call on the church to discern how to walk that distinctive way in whatever situation we find ourselves. The ethics of Christ's body isn't about right and wrong according to a set of moral principles but about discerning the kind of work the Spirit is enlivening the body to do as part of the renewal of creation.

When we find ourselves out of step with the way of Jesus, the hard work of confession and repentance redemptively allows us to walk the way of new creation. From churches happily filling buildings not far from Nazi concentration camps in the 1940s to the way that the cross has often been a symbol of terror, hate, and exclusion across the North American landscape over the past two centuries, we have seen that not all work Christians have done or are doing is the work of Christ's body. Failure to do the work of Christ's body is a painful reality for a church that gathers in a fallen creation, but it is a reality that must be acknowledged and confessed so the repentant work of Christ's body can be done.

John Wesley saw the need for this kind of work when he began a reform movement in England that came to be called Methodism. Focused on the possibilities of new creation breaking into the old and fueled by the pursuit of the more excellent way, Wesley set up gatherings of Christians in small groups in hopes that the Spirit would use those groups to move the body of Christ into service faithfully. Made up of people from various churches and denominations, the largest of these groups was called a "society." There were also "classes" of twelve people, and the still more intimate "bands" that we've already examined. Although each of these gatherings took a slightly different form, all served the purpose of enlivening the church across England to do the holy work of Christ's body.

One of the aspects that was most striking about these gatherings was that they cut across social boundary lines, as discussed in chapter 4. The rich and the poor were included in the same groups, and those who wielded lots of social power sat beside those who lived at the outskirts of society's circle. Those desiring to take the step into a band needed to answer a series of questions, including this one: "Do you desire to be told of your faults?" It's hard to imagine many people seeking out a venue where your faults can be pointed out in front of other people, but for those who signed on, the benefits were worth the discomfort. These people came to seek a life of holy love, and if their faults were getting in the way of that goal, having their faults illuminated was a small price to pay. What I don't want us to miss is that when the powerful sat next to those who had no power, they were giving permission to have their faults pointed out by those same powerless people. Imagine a wealthy factory owner sitting alongside a man who worked in the factory. In this setting, a possibility would be open for the worker to say to the owner, "What I saw you do yesterday was contrary to the body of Christ. It didn't reflect God's image. I point that out because you may not be able to see it, but I can see it, and I thought you'd like to know." The point was never for the worker to try to take the owner down a notch for his own satisfaction but for the owner and the worker to come together to spur one another on to reflect the image of God more fully and to live a holy life.

The possibility Wesley saw in these kinds of associations was nothing short of new creation. It was nothing short of holiness. If a church is going to be set apart for God's work alone—which is one way of describing holiness—this was the kind of thing that would allow the church to discern and do the work of Christ's body. Wesley knew we needed to open ourselves to associations with people who care enough to lovingly speak into the places where the image of God may be distorted by the kind of work we are doing—and then ask them to do the same for us. This is the kind of association that opens to us not only the possibility of holiness but also of *freedom*. These kinds of associations would probably make most people think of lots of things when they hear about them, but freedom probably isn't near the top of the list. Most of the time, modern folks tend to associate freedom with the *lack* of people reminding us of our faults. When we hear the word "freedom," we usually think of a life where no one can call us out, no one can tell us what to do, and we are at liberty to do whatever we want. In many ways, this is the modern vision of the good life.

For the Christian faith, though, it tends to be a vision of misery. Lacking associations with other people is a form of isolation that can lead us to turn inward upon ourselves. Martin Luther's classic definition of the sinner is a person turned in upon the self, a kind of anthropological feedback loop. It is the life of a person whose desires, impulses, and actions serve themselves. They think of themselves, act for themselves, and make themselves the focus of their life. In short, their self-focus becomes a kind of prison, trapping them in a life no bigger than their own self. Here we can begin to see how associations with others, even those who ask pressing questions, offer the possibility of freely doing the work of Christ's body. I'm fond of the way Robert Jenson addresses freedom: "Freedom occurs only in the meeting of *persons*," he says. "It is only when I meet someone different from me, and only if in that meeting I am *challenged*, that I might possibly become someone different from the person I already am. Freedom is a possibility for me, but it is not something that I possess; it is something that *occurs* when at least two persons pose new possibilities to one another."[2]

There is no escaping it, and hopefully we wouldn't want to. The Spirit is breathing the body of Christ to freely do the work of new creation in the world, and the Spirit often uses the voices of others to help us repent of the times when we have been less than free in our work. Hopefully the joy and freedom of working as Christ's body will encourage us in the work of listening, hearing, confessing, and repenting so that the church's work can truly be free to work the more excellent way of *Christ's* body. Such is the work that is done in hope.

Working in Hope

"Hope" is also a loaded word that we'll need to relieve of its common understanding if we are to understand how the body of Christ's work is hopeful. Hope is not wishful thinking about a future possibility. Rather, it is work done in light of a reality that has not yet come in its fullness. It is doing the work *now* in light of the reality that has yet to be completed. Theologians often refer to this kind of hope as *eschatological* hope. Since that's not a familiar term to most, perhaps a story will help.

I was teaching a theology course several years ago that met early in the morning. All semester, the students had been attentive and engaged, but toward the end, the limits of the flesh began to overtake some of the willingness of the spirit. About halfway through a discussion on eschatological hope one morning, I saw a student on the back row give up her fight with fatigue, put her head down on the desk, and go straight to sleep. It was a moment I couldn't have planned on my best day. "Some of you may be wishing

2. Robert W. Jenson, *A Theology in Outline: Can These Bones Live?* (New York: Oxford University Press, 2016), 87.

right now that this class was over, and you may be *hoping* to return to your rooms for a morning nap," I said. "That's not eschatological hope, though. Wishful thinking about the future isn't eschatology. Eschatological hope is living *now* as if that reality has already dawned. When it comes to eschatological hope," I said, motioning to the slumbering student, "I think only one of us here truly gets it."

Like a student who didn't wait until class was over to take a nap, the church doesn't wait to do the work of new creation. Convinced that God has already opened the door to new creation by opening the tomb for Jesus, the church works new creation realities today, even though the new creation hasn't yet come in its fullness. When the church gathers for worship, we aren't thinking wishfully about what God will do but are actively working out what God has done—that which was inaugurated in Christ Jesus and will come to fulfillment upon Christ's return.

Christian Worship as Rehearsal of New Creation

What might it look like to approach Christian worship as an eschatological rehearsal of new creation? We are a people who live so perpetually in the old creation that an eschatological approach to worship will be necessary to awaken us to the realities of new creation. The concluding chapters of Revelation offer a compelling image of worship in the new creation that deals with the liturgical elements of worship space, singing, power dynamics, and the direction of adoration. The dazzling image John conveys of this new creation includes a world set to the pattern and life of a God who dwells with the people as a Slaughtered Lamb. Evidenced by his wounds, old creation had its way with this Lamb, yet his pattern of love and self-sacrifice turns out to be the true way the world is made new. Everyone else in this city is oriented to this Lamb, and a river flowing from the Lamb's throne gives life to the whole new creation (Rev. 22:1). The kings lead their nations into this grand city, not in war as kings have done throughout old creation's history, but in praise and peace (21:24). Everything about this city demonstrates that humans have been reconciled to God, to one another, and to the rest of the creation. They delight in God's presence, and the earth freely provides food for all.

Such a vision is obviously not fully realized in our world, which is precisely why the church's worship could offer something truly different to old creation if it were to tune its work to the song of new creation. If our liturgical practices invite only a rehearsal of the old creation, the potency of the church's moral vision will begin to dissipate. Worship as an eschatological rehearsal celebrates the reality of new creation and shapes us to be able to work according to its dynamics. It prepares us, week after week, to work the dynamics of new creation in the midst of the old, and to confess our failures to do so. In ethical terms, it forms within us the kind of *ethos*, or character, of a people who are aligned toward new creation. A people who *practice* new creation week in and week out will be formed to be able to do the work of new creation in the everyday lives they lead. The more excellent way can become the normal way we walk.

Consider how Christian worship can draw us into the dynamics of God's future. Consider how it is, in a sense, joining the liturgy of the New Jerusalem, in which the Slaughtered Lamb is at the center of all that is done. Consider how a weekly practice of worship could help us practice being aligned with Christ's distinct way of working. Consider how worship could be a means of grace for a people to leave behind secondary commitments and alignments and cast off every crown of the old creation before the throne of the Slaughtered Lamb. A people who are made capable of doing that are a people who can be active in the midst of old creation, walking the way of Christ, even if it costs them everything. This is why the eschato-logical ethics of new creation are far more than wishful thinking—they are hopeful living. The body of Christ at work is called by God and empowered by the Spirit to be a vision and real embodiment of the future God is giving to the world.

A "royal priesthood," as Peter has it (1 Pet. 2:9), is meant to mediate God's redemptive presence to the world, but that kind of work will require a set of practices that will free them to do that kind of work. Imagine the hope of those who "were not a people" becoming "the people of God" (v. 10) by the power of the Spirit and beginning to do the work of Christ's new creation body in the world—precisely because they'd been rehearsing the new creation's dynamics for years. And when that work begins to happen, a vision of new creation begins to dawn upon our moral imagination. In the furtive ways that the Spirit breathes new creation to life in the everyday realities of the world, the church will begin to breathe, its limbs begin to move, and its heart begin to beat in rhythm with New Jerusalem's song of praise to the crucified and risen Christ.

Discerning the Work of
Christian Ethics

Part II

Discernment Dialogue 1
Biomedical Ethics

"If you had been here," Mary fires at Jesus with what I imagine is more than a little bit of anger, "my brother would not have died" (John 11:21). Mary's frustration born of her grief is something most of us can probably relate to, especially if we have spent any time living in that thin place between life and death. Recalling my own memories of sitting in a hospital room beside a loved one and listening to the hums and beeps of the medical equipment, I can't help but wonder if the human impulse to develop such technologies is to call out with Mary in the desperation of helplessness, "Where are you? My loved one is dying, and you aren't here!"

The moral questions surrounding biomedical ethics are some of the most complex that we face in contemporary society. Medical technologies are emerging and developing at such a rapid pace that whatever technologies or treatments I name here will be outdated by the time this book is in your hands. Each treatment and technology is additionally complicated. Stem cell research, fertility hormone therapy, pre-implantation genetic diagnosis, organ transplantation, and the use and production of medications, for example, are all different forms of treatment and cannot be lumped together in one question that can then be decisively answered. Rather than attempt to peel back the layers of complexity for even one of these issues, I find it helpful in our discernment to consider two general criteria that are at home in a Wesleyan formulation of Christian ethics and closely related to one another. The first is the notion of becoming a right-hearted person, and the second is a moral orientation toward the new creation that God is bringing.

Being right-hearted is not about being sentimental or romantic. It is to have one's heart aligned toward God's new creation purposes. Most of the time, our on-the-ground and beside-the-bed decisions have to be made without the guidance of an entirely clear path. Medical professionals will offer us an array of options, and may be able to advise which path they would recommend, but in view of the reality that medicine is as much an art as it is a science, our hearts will be called upon to do a lot of the ethical lifting. The question then becomes how our hearts have been aligned. To what end are they aimed, especially when we are making biomedical decisions?

On top of these complexities is the reality that the continual proliferation of biomedical technologies plays games with our hearts. To be sure, medical science has been an invaluable partner in the flourishing of God's creation. It has alleviated suffering and preserved life, and against these things we have no quarrel. At the same time, each new technology that arrives comes whispering serpentine promises that it will never be able to keep: *You can use me to take power over aging. You can use me to stop all illness. You can overcome your finitude if you use me. You can take control. You can even stop death. I can bring this chaos under control.*

What *are* biomedical technologies and treatments if not the attempt to bring chaos under control? Rogue cell mutations are brought to heel by powerful chemotherapies; malfunctioning organ systems are reestablished to order by transplant; infertile wombs can be made fruitful; even the body's out-of-order reaction to springtime pollen can be righted through medication. The short version of the biomedical story is that we can make use of treatments and technologies to bring disorder under control. In perhaps the most modern of all moral phenomena, even if we accept the finitude of our bodies, we can still seek to use medical technology to take control over the time and means of our deaths.

On one hand, establishing order in the midst of chaos is right out of the book of Genesis. New creation purposes can't be far behind. The New Jerusalem doesn't have need for a temple because of God's ubiquitous presence, so it likely doesn't need a hospital either. The moral question has to do with when we are using biomedical technology to live in the garden, and when we are using it to reach for the apple. Knowing the difference is most likely a matter of the heart's aim. Is our application of biomedical technology tuned toward the flourishing of life, or has it become an attempt to take control of death? Parsing the lines between those two options will never be a clear-cut enterprise, but perhaps we can gain some discernment help by returning to the Gospel accounts of Jesus's ministry, especially regarding sickness. Jesus clearly does not have a problem with healing those who are in need, and he offers a healing touch to many. When John the Baptist requests confirmation from Jesus about his identity, Jesus says to the disciples John has sent, "Go back and report to John what you hear and see: The blind receive sight, the lame walk, those who have leprosy are cleansed, the deaf hear, the dead are raised, and the good news is proclaimed to the poor" (Matt. 11:4–5). Apparently the kingdom Jesus is bringing includes the healing of illness.

At the same time, the Gospels tell us that Jesus's ministry of healing is not a desperate attempt to flee death at all costs. Upon receiving the news of his friend Lazarus's illness, he lingers, not rushing to his friend's side (John 11:6). When Lazarus does die, Jesus is clearly upset, which seems odd. If Jesus knew of the sickness and had the capacity to heal it, why not rush to the side of his ailing friend? There may be a hint here about Jesus's relationship

The moral question has to do with when we are using biomedical technology to live in the garden, and when we are using it to reach for the apple.

to death: he is deeply saddened by it and perhaps wishes it had not occurred, but he also engages it as a reality that will not have the last word; thus, he does not have to strain against it in desperation. "This sickness will not end in death," he tells his followers (v. 4). Lazarus, of course, does die, and his death moves Jesus to tears. Yet Jesus does not engage frantically. He does not rush to his friend. Death, as Jesus appears to handle it, is a heart-wrenching reality to be grieved, and it is something that will be overcome in the resurrection, but it is not something he engages in a desperate attempt to take control. Although death does not have the last word over Lazarus, it is a reality Jesus seems to tearfully accept when it comes to his friend.

Additionally, Jesus seems more interested in restoring Lazarus to life, rather than simply holding off death. In the presence of medical technologies that allow us, in some instances, to force human bodies to continue to function, perhaps we can be reminded by Jesus that the application of healing is for life, not merely to delay death a bit longer. Recalling this story from the bedside of a loved one I have to wonder if my desire for Jesus to come near is only for the sake of being able to prevent death. Perhaps my motivation in that moment is to do anything I can to prevent someone I love from dying, and I would stop at nothing to hold death at bay. And perhaps when Jesus doesn't show up in time, my anger explodes: "What held you up? Why wouldn't you pull out all the stops to prevent him from dying?" In that moment, I need to reckon with this reality: Jesus doesn't seem to want to prevent death at all costs. He is no friend of death, and nothing in him delights in it. He heals those who are in need, and he even brings the dead back to life! Still, we search the Gospels in vain to find an account of Jesus desperately doing anything and everything to prevent death from occurring. Even when his own life hangs in the balance,

Jesus resists anything that looks like the impulse to take control so that he simply wouldn't have to die.

What Jesus does instead is enter into death and come out on the other side, opening to us a new reality in which we can do the work of moral discernment. Death is no longer the ultimate reality that governs the work of ethics. Rather, it is the life of new creation, and we orient our moral discernment toward that reality. Death is a distinct and undeniable reality of the human experience, but even so, it will not ultimately overcome the life God has granted; so the moral point is pressed to us in hope: we can make biomedical decisions by entrusting our loved ones and ourselves into the new creation God is bringing. None of this is easy, of course. Even Jesus struggles to entrust his future to the Father, and when he finally does, he is not prevented from dying (Matt. 26:38–39). The Father, though, returns to the Son a resurrected future that doesn't prevent death but offers a life on the other side of death that will never be squelched again. The future given to us by God is one in which death is defeated but not yet prevented. The martyrs who died as victims of the old creation are resurrected into the new creation and can be identified by the method of their death (Rev. 20:4–6).

The moral vision guiding our discernment is one in which healing is sought but death is no longer the ultimate reality that must be avoided at all costs. Like Jesus, we align our lives to the new creation, mournfully accept death when it comes, and entrust our future to the new creation God is opening to us. In this view, medical treatments and technologies can be aimed at restoring life, rather than frantically holding off death. This moral vision runs counter to most modern morality, however. We are people who try to take most things under our control through the application of biomedical technology. The philosophical river of modernity has been cutting a deep moral canyon for hundreds of years. How might we climb out of the canyon to become the kinds of people who align our hearts toward new creation aims?

The Christian life is shaped by the faith to give one's life to the way of Jesus. It is taking cues from the one we follow, and the act of following is what packs the moral punch. In the very act of following, disciples proclaim that their lives are not theirs to be entirely self-possessed or self-directed. Discipleship runs counter to the impulse to dictate the course of one's own life. Disciples have learned the art of living in the world as those who do not seek to control it, even as they offer and receive healing. The Wesleyan view of salvation helps align our hearts to be the kinds of disciples who aren't out to take biomedical control over our finitude. Sometimes described as a *via salutis*, the Wesleyan vision of salvation is, as the Latin phrase suggests, a way of health! Even our word *"salvation"* has healing at its root—a salve is meant to heal. Perhaps God's work of salvation also includes healing our hearts from the moral wounds inflicted by the temptation to control.

We return to the moral question that guides this short excursus. What guides our bedside decisions on the use of biomedical treatments? Is it a desire to take control over a situation, or is it a desire for the restoration of health, a glimpse of God's original intent for creation's flourishing? Will this treatment serve the purpose of restoring a loved one to health, or is it simply a desperate attempt to prevent death? Obviously, these lines are not always clear, and there is no biological marker that signifies whether *this* treatment will heal someone we love. But the way of Jesus calls to us in the midst of these decisions. It gently reminds us that the one we follow is no friend of death, but neither did he struggle against it in desperation. His calling to us was always a call to dispossess ourselves of grasping greedily onto the things and people we love, and to entrust them into God's care.

Biomedical ethics is not only about end-of-life matters, of course, and much of what I've developed here regarding the temptation to control applies to the beginning of life as well. Given the biomedical options at our disposal and the language we now use to describe "making babies," the technology whispers again: *You can have whatever you want.* The attunement of our hearts will guide our response. Will we wield fertility treatments in service to our will to have something we want, or will we approach them as an opportunity for life to flourish? If the former, our moral vision may behold the child as an object, rather than a gift gratefully received and stewarded well. We are not making claims here about the rightness or wrongness of fertility treatments but raising a point of moral discernment: to what end is the heart aimed as we consider the use of this technology?

The procedures and technologies surrounding gene editing or stem cells may also be a movement toward healing, but they could likewise be an attempt to shake our fist in answer to Mary's angry question. Generally, I find it helpful when considering the morality of these kinds of technologies to ask whether the application is toward healing or if it serves as a frustrated and controlling response to do whatever we hoped Jesus would do but didn't. Does this treatment find a faithful place in the pattern of the one who gave a healing touch to those in need, or does it ring more like the biomedical statement, "Fine! If you won't show up, then I'm going to do something about this myself!"

Admittedly, this line of questioning is not designed to offer clear and irrefutable answers to on-the-ground and beside-the-bed questions of whether *this* or *that* particular treatment is morally permissible. It does, however, open a line of examination whereby followers of Christ might be able to scrutinize our *motivations* for making such decisions. Consider what kind of people we are becoming as we make biomedical decisions according to certain motivations. What kind of people will we become once we've begun to use therapies as an attempt to become masters of the garden? I suspect that a character formed over a lifetime of intentionally following Jesus would produce the kind of character in a person who would turn away from treatments that move beyond care and toward control. I suspect those kinds of persons would be able to know the difference between healing and dominion when the options are presented to them, even if they aren't able to articulate the difference. Perhaps, in the face of such options, they are the ones who relieve themselves of the choice to attempt to take control, and follow faithfully the path of Christ, offering their futures to the care of God.

Questions for Discernment

1) In this particular situation, are we attempting to bring healing or take control?
2) To what degree will this medical procedure or application of technology bring healing? To what degree will it be used to evade death?
3) To what degree is this application of biomedical technology the work of new creation? How much is it trying to control old creation?

Resources for Further Exploration

Hauerwas, Stanley. *God, Medicine, and Suffering*. Grand Rapids: William. B. Eerdmans Publishing Company 1990.

Meilander, Gilbert. *Bioethics: A Primer for Christians*. Third Edition. Grand Rapids: William B. Eerdmans Publishing Company, 2013.

Waters, Brent. *This Mortal Flesh: Incarnation and Bioethics*. Grand Rapids: Brazos Press, 2009.

Discernment Dialogue 2
Technology and Ethics

Perhaps more than any other force shaping our time, technology shapes our moral lives. Most of life is mediated to us through technology, whether you happen to read an eBook, talk on the phone, or access news online. All of that is bound to shape the way we think about our relationship to the world around us as well as the way we act in relationship to the world. In this short reflection, I'd like to offer a brief account of technology, describe some of its moral implications, and offer some questions that will allow you and your community to continue the process of discernment together on how technology might be used well by a people who seek *orthokardia*.

In seeking to be right-hearted, the moral vision of technology I offer isn't one that assumes electronics fall automatically into a bad moral category while all things that came before backlit screens and the internet are good. Frankly, those moral categories are too simplistic when it comes to how we think about technology as people who seek *orthokardia*. Rather than producing a list of what should be allowed and not allowed when it comes to technology, I'd like to explore what the constant and pervasive use of technology is doing to us. I want to raise questions about the kind of *ethos*—the kind of character—our use of technology is producing.

Most of the time, I suspect we equate technology with electronics. While these devices are certainly included, technological forces existed long before computers, smartphones, and the internet. Technology is any device or mechanism that allows the claims being made upon us to be reduced. Technology is the network of devices and systems that makes life cheaper, quicker, and easier. Certainly this definition applies to electronics. A cell phone reduces the claim that a thousand miles of distance makes on you when you want to talk with a loved one. You simply pick up the phone, allowing you to overcome that distance instantly. Mobile banking technology (one of my particular favorites) makes it possible for me to deposit checks, pay bills, and check balances without making a trip to the bank to wait in line. If I need a toaster, I can go to a store that specializes in appliances, or I turn to the internet, select the least expensive option from numerous models, and have it delivered to my doorstep a couple of days—or, in some cases, hours—later.

I'm not trying to say there's an inherent moral message in any of the choices from these examples. What I am trying to say is that the everyday technology we use whispers a moral message to us: *If it's quicker, cheaper, and easier, it's automatically better.* Often, this is followed up with a related message: *You shouldn't have to be claimed by something that's going to take up your time, energy, or resources. If something is doing that, technology can fix it.* Our pervasive use of technology has offered us a vision of the good life that is defined by being unclaimed by life's difficulties.

When I was fairly young, probably about seven or eight years old, I sat down at the dinner table at my grandparents' house. They lived on a small farm, where they grew and sold walnuts, but they also had a vegetable garden that served the family. That evening, my grandmother placed a steaming bowl of broccoli on the table, harvested about an hour before from the garden thirty yards from where we gathered to eat it.

"It must be great to have a garden like this," I said to her, "so you can just go get whatever you want, any time you want it!"

She laughed loudly and replied, "You think that's how it works, huh?"

Of course, if you have ever planted and maintained a vegetable garden, you can understand why she laughed. When I looked at the garden, I saw that it was just *there*, ready for the picking. But my grandmother saw that garden differently. She saw the labor-intensive practice of preparing the ground, planting, watering, weeding, maintaining, and harvesting—all in the heat of a California summer. Nothing about getting that broccoli to the table was quick, cheap, or easy.

I contrast that memory with the way I consume broccoli now. It begins by pulling into the parking lot of a grocery store on my way home from work. I have the option of using a smartphone to order and pay for it online (choosing the brand that was on sale, of course), so I find the designated parking space to wait. While I sit in my air-conditioned car, an industrious grocery store employee appears at my window, hands me a plastic bag of pre-cut broccoli, and wishes me a good day. That bag was probably transported to the store a few days earlier by a sophisticated system of logistics that used automated cutting machinery, assembly-line packaging, and refrigerated trucking. I take the bag home, microwave it for a few minutes, and have it ready to serve without thinking twice about how technological that broccoli really is. Everything about that transaction was cheaper, quicker, and easier than what my grandmother did. But was it *good*? Does its being cheaper, quicker, and easier mean it was *better*? There's no doubt that technology is lifting financial and logistical burdens in the food-production industry, but it raises a moral question: what kind of person am I becoming when I bypass the claims that would be made on me if I were to grow my own broccoli? What moral character did my grandmother possess through her ongoing effort at tilling the soil, getting up early to tend the garden, and harvesting at just the right time? What kind of person did she become through those actions, and will I ever possess the same character traits that grew out of her hard work in that plot of soil in the middle of California? She was a farmer. I'm a consumer.

For people seeking to pattern their lives in the way of Jesus Christ, the moral implications are pressing. If our moral vision has equated goodness with things being cheaper, quicker, and easier, what do we do with a gospel that is anything but quick, cheap, and easy? We should not shy away from it: the gospel of Jesus will make claims on us. It will make claims on our desires, our resources, our bodies, our money, and every other aspect of life. If that sentence strikes you as uncomfortably as it strikes me, perhaps it's because the ubiquitous presence of technology in our lives has made the idea of having any part of ourselves be claimed seem distasteful.

Discipleship—the moral shape of the Christian life—is a life of being claimed by Jesus Christ. Those claims are costly, and there are no technological shortcuts around them. Following Jesus makes claims on our time, our resources, and our energy, and those costly claims are *good*. As a technological people, have we developed an allergy to being claimed? Has our pervasive use of technology that can "solve the problem" of being claimed shaped us into people who see the claim of Jesus Christ upon us as unnecessarily burdensome and problematic? If this is the case, what could Christians do to understand the claim of Christ not as a problem but as a gracious reality of the Christian life? Perhaps we need to relearn how to be claimed. Perhaps we need to find practices and habits that are central to the

Christian life and lean hard into them, precisely because they make claims upon us.

In addressing the challenge of moral formation in a technological age, philosopher Albert Borgmann suggests that communities need "focal things" and "focal practices" that allow us to celebrate well. Focal things and focal practices are objects or routines that focus the community's attention and resources by unapologetically making claims on the members of that community.[1] In a soccer team, for example, the soccer ball is a focal thing, and their daily drills are focal practices. Gathering every afternoon to work out, learn skills, and gain athletic competence makes claims on the players' time, energy, and resources. Hours of hard work go into learning how to kick the ball and pass it to other players, so while a soccer ball may not be able to speak or act on its own, it still makes demands upon those who choose to pursue the sport. While the hours of practice that a team puts in might seem mundane, consider what it looks like to watch that team win a hard-fought game. Their capacity to celebrate that victory is given to them by the claims focal practice made on their time, their effort, and their resources.

The question for Christian ethics is what kind of focal practices lie at the center of Christian communities. What kind of claim-making practices might allow us to gain a capacity to celebrate deeply because we've known what it is to be claimed by the way of Jesus? A children's Bible-quizzing team gains a capacity to celebrate Scripture because it has become a focal thing in their lives as they've spent hours reading and memorizing. Musicians increase their capacity to celebrate because they take the time and effort to learn their instruments well. In the Christian communi-

---

1. Albert Borgmann, *Power Failure: Christianity in the Culture of Technology* (Grand Rapids: Brazos Press, 2003).

ty, the Eucharist can be a focal practice *par excellence*. Odd as it may be to say that we celebrate such a somber event as Christ's body and blood being broken and poured out, we do so precisely because it is a costly event. The gifts of bread and cup come to us at God's incredible expense. They are not quick, cheap, or easy.

As these costly gifts of divine love take a central place in our communal life, they may give birth to more costly practices that shape the kind of people we are. We may find that sacrificing our time and resources becomes central to who we are. Not far from where I live, a rural congregation has committed to giving away at least half their church's annual income. Another nearby church runs an afterschool program for students who need extra help with academic and life skills. Giving away income is costly, and there's nothing quick about mentoring children, but that's exactly why these practices have become points of celebration and life for these communities. If these ministries were quick, cheap, or easy, it's doubtful they would have much capacity to shape the character of a people.

In your own community, what things and practices call for deep commitment? Perhaps they are a primary reality in the way you are being shaped morally. Even in an age of technology, Christians can still learn to be people of *orthokardia* whose hearts are aligned to Jesus's way because they do not shirk the claims Christ is making on them but welcome those claims as a means of redemptive grace to truly celebrate new creation.

Questions for Discernment

1) What is the relationship between what is good and what is cheap, quick, or easy?
2) What Christian practices can you think of that make claims on our time, resources, and ener-

gy that might help us live into the claims Christ makes on us?

3) How do you think allowing these kinds of claims aids us in being right-hearted (*orthokardia*) people?

4) How do you think some of these practices could be enacted in your local context?

Resources for Further Exploration

Borgmann, Albert. *Power Failure: Christianity in the Culture of Technology*. Grand Rapids: Brazos Press, 2003.

Ott, Kate. *Christian Ethics for a Digital Society*. Lanham, MD: Rowman & Littlefield, 2019.

Discernment Dialogue 3
Economic Ethics

A Wesleyan approach to economic ethics begins at the end. We take account of the new creation and the kind of reality God is bringing about in the world, and then we work to align toward that reality. We ask both "As I am made new, how are my desires related to finite resources being reoriented?" and "What kind of reality is God bringing about in the world, and how can I use resources accordingly?"

Let's begin with the vision we find in the final two chapters of Revelation. For the sake of economic ethics, I'll highlight a few of the salient parts. "It is done," John hears the Lord say as he catches a glimpse of the new creation. "I am the Alpha and the Omega, the Beginning and the End. To the thirsty I will give water without cost from the spring of the water of life" (21:6). In the next chapter, this promise is delivered. "Then the angel showed me the river of the water of life, as clear as crystal, flowing from the throne of God and of the Lamb down the middle of the great street of the city. On each side of the river stood the tree of life, bearing twelve crops of fruit, yielding its fruit every month. And the leaves of the tree are for the healing of the nations" (Rev. 22:1–2). From the very heart of the new creation, God's provision flows. A stream of life-giving water flows directly from the throne, giving life and offering healing. This is the vision for the economic ethics of new creation.

So far, I haven't equated economic ethics with the use of *money* alone, mainly because economic ethics is about more than just money. It's about the kind of interplay and exchange that allow creation to flourish. The aim of economic ethics is the kind of exchange that flows from God and brings flourishing and healing to the whole creation. It is a reorientation from the sentiment "I earned this, and I'm going to do whatever I want with it" to something like, "This is a gift from God, and I'd like to use it in a way that helps the world." In short, we move from being possessors to being stewards.

Becoming a faithful steward is an image Jesus prefers in his parables. It's the notion of receiving what has been entrusted to us and using it in a way that opens new possibilities and realities not only for ourselves but also for our neighbors and the rest of creation. It is taking a cue from the biblical vision of new creation and asking, "How can we join in the flow that comes from the throne of God and use it for the sake of healing the nations?" Hopefully these are the kinds of questions that lift economic ethics out of categories of legalism or the brackets of income levels. In the economy of the new creation, all persons can participate, and all can benefit.

Oliver O'Donovan, a contemporary theological ethicist, has developed economic ethics in terms of communication. This is a term that isn't simply the transmission of information from one person to another. O'Donovan notes that "communication" shares a root and a purpose with the terms "common" and "community." Economically, communication takes place in the way goods are held and stewarded so that a common good is upheld in the midst of a community. This communication "is the good of the community of communicating members, consisting in their capacity to realise fulfillment *through* living together."[1] Piercing the prose,

---

1. Oliver O'Donovan, "Communicating the Good: The Politics and Ethics of 'The Common Good,'" *ABC Religion and Ethics*, https://www.abc.net.au/

O'Donovan signals here that the joy of stewarding resources is being able to use them in a way that brings life. This isn't to say that individuals are deprived of their goods or have their goods taken from them, but it is to say we view the goods that have been entrusted to us for the sake of a common good, rather than a strictly individual one.

Perhaps there is some significance that O'Donovan worked out the finer points of this economic ethics while he was a professor at the University of Oxford, where John Wesley trained for ministry and worked out the first versions of his own economic ethics. There Wesley gathered with a small group to pursue the more excellent way of holiness, where one question they posed to themselves and others was whether they prayed about how they spent money. Wesley's well-known mantra regarding economic ethics was, "Having, first, gained all you can and, secondly, saved all you can, then give all you can."[2] Gaining resources was meant to be done without causing harm to self or others, and saving had to do with cutting off frivolous, unnecessary expenses. The rest, Wesley taught, went to God. As an Oxford-educated member of the clergy, Wesley fell into one of the higher-income brackets of his day, yet he spent time begging for money from others so he might give it to those in need after he had exhausted his own resources. Though he gained a substantial income, he saved through an exacting limitation of spending on many needless comforts and was accustomed to giving whatever he had to those in need.

While we tend to the pragmatics of Wesley's economic ethics we shouldn't lose sight of the theological currents in which Wesley's economic ethics was carried. Wesley viewed

---

religion/communicating-the-good-the-politics-and-ethics-of-the-common-goo/10096290. See also O'Donovan's *The Ways of Judgment* (Grand Rapids: William B. Eerdmans Publishing Company, 2005) and *Finding and Seeking: Ethics as Theology* (Grand Rapids: William B. Eerdmans Publishing Company, 2014).

2. Wesley, "The Use of Money," *Works.*

money as "an opportunity of grace to do good, to respond to God's gifts in a way fitting to their temporal and limited value."[3] The good toward which our use of money could be aimed was nothing short of new creation. When the Holy Spirit gets ahold of human motivation, Wesley argued, it not only makes that person a new creation, but it also steers them to use their goods in service to the way God is making all things new. "At Pentecost the church was experiencing a new birth of Spirit, recognizing the new creation that springs from Jesus's death and resurrection and the coming of the Spirit."[4]

Wesley's optimistic moral view was that human motivation could be turned toward using our resources for the sake of this new creation. Pastorally, Wesley aimed at the "training of the moral imagination and reasoning [in order to] develop character that uses money for sharing God's love through mercy and charitable acts for the needy."[5] Returning to the imagery of Revelation, whatever is flowing toward the city emerges from the wellspring of God. As those who are aligned to the realities of the new creation, we not only receive the goods of life as such, but we also handle them in such a way that they become a means of God's grace to others. The work of ethics is to tune our hearts to that reality, shaping our character in such a way that handling these resources becomes second nature for a new creation people.

Although all of this may appear well and good, how does it help us discern well as we sit with questions of economic ethics or face difficult decisions regarding finite resources? I can see this landing in a local church setting in any number of ways, but I'll reserve my comments for a few.

---

3. Thomas C. Oden, *John Wesley's Teachings: Issues of Ethics and Society* (Grand Rapids: Zondervan, 2012), 60.

4. Oden, *John Wesley's Teachings*, 62.

5. Oden, *John Wesley's Teachings*, 60.

The aim of economic ethics is the kind of exchange that flows from God and brings flourishing and healing to the whole creation.

First, in the midst of increasing political diversity in congregations, this new creation approach may be able to confound the categories that often hold people apart from one another on economic grounds. While questions of tax policy and international monetary policy are not to be ignored, perhaps conceiving of economic ethics as a means of participation in new creation offers us a different way to have that conversation. Perhaps questions like, "What is the best way for resources to be used to allow more flourishing?" will move us beyond the well-worn debates over conservative and liberal economic principles. Indeed, it does not answer the question I've just posed, but at least it turns the conversation toward the use of resources as a means of grace, rather than a means of securing our own wealth. This is not to say private ownership ought to disappear as a matter of necessity, but it is to say that whatever private ownership is moves toward a purpose beyond itself. "The private interest must first be located within the common interest," O'Donovan argues. "The 'I' find its context within the 'we.'"[6]

Moving the heart and forming the character toward new creation ends is no small thing. Perhaps this is why Jesus is quick to acknowledge riches as a barrier to entering the kingdom of new creation. Wesley, too, toiled pastorally to move those in his care away from serving themselves alone with their money. This opens to another question of economic ethics in the local church setting, and that is tithing. Hopefully the Wesleyan vision of economic ethics can turn the giving of resources to the church from legalistic categories of percentages toward joyful participation in new creation. What if tithing were about offering what has been entrusted to us to God's work of healing the nations? If the church is where new creation is happening, it seems a natural place to invest resources.

6. O'Donovan, "Communicating the Good."

This, then, immediately poses another question: what is the church doing with the resources it receives? Is it ordering its own economic life toward new creation, or has the local church begun to serve itself with the resources that have been entrusted into its care? The unfortunate reality is that we are prone to build a dam on the river that flows from the throne of God, diverting resources to places and purposes that do less than providing for the flourishing of creation and the healing of nations. The more excellent way of economic ethics calls local churches to carefully consider how they steward the resources they receive. Pastorally, I have found that prayer before an offering is an opportune time to ask for God's help in aligning our purposes to the new creation so that whatever is about to be entrusted to the church will be used in a more excellent way.

Questions for Discernment

1) As we consider this decision, to what ultimate end are our resources being used?
2) How have we built dams on the river of life of new creation? How have we diverted resources meant to heal creation toward some other purpose?
3) How is my own understanding of resources aligned or not aligned with God's purpose of making the world new? What practices can I put into place to begin shaping my character toward that reality?

Resources for Further Exploration

Jennings, Theodore W. *Good News to the Poor: John Wesley's Evangelical Economics*. Nashville: Abingdon Press, 1990.

Tanner, Kathryn. *Christianity and the New Spirit of Capitalism*. New Haven, CT: Yale University Press, 2019.

Waters, Brent. *Just Capitalism: A Christian Ethic of Economic Globalization*. Louisville: Westminster John Knox Press, 2016.

Discernment Dialogue 4
Political Ethics

Political ethics in the church suffers from a lack of imagination. The primary challenge, at least in a North American context,[1] is that political ethics in the church often operates within the categories that are given to it. There isn't anything particularly distinct about the political conversations being had in the church. If any community is called to and capable of engaging political ethics differently, it should be the church. The gospel of Christ and the good news of his resurrection—a way of life, rather than a series of ideas—is a distinct kind of politics in itself.

When I use the term "politics," I'm not talking about the partisan back-and-forth, or the divisive bickering that's often in mind when one says, "I don't want to get political." My use of the term points to the art of arranging persons, goods, institutions, and services in ways that open a path for good purposes. Of course, the way we come to the decisions about how these realities ought to be arranged rarely comes without some amount of discussion or deliberation. The failure of these deliberations to produce these ends, or the failure to remember what those ends are supposed to

---

1. A wider engagement of political life and Christian ethics is not possible in a reflection of this length. I have opted to engage the context in which I do my work and have my ecclesial life. At the same time, I have taken a scope in this excursus that I hope will also offer relevant reflections to those outside the American context.

be, characterizes so much of our politics today. This being the case, I want to set aside some of the common questions associated with politics, such as, "What should a Christian stance be on this particular issue?" or "How should a Christian vote?" Questions like these need to be navigated in community and deliberated honestly in the company of those who seek to follow Jesus faithfully and who will press us to do the same. If we set those questions aside for the time being, perhaps a new set of questions may be helpful to local communities who seek to discern faithful steps in the way of Jesus when it comes to politics. These are questions having to do with what we are attempting to do with our engagement of politics, and whether a distinction between political engagement as *anticipation* and political engagement as *hope* makes any difference.

Both anticipation and hope have an eye to the future, but in different ways. When we anticipate the future, we have a particular outcome in mind. Those outcomes are often associated with a fairly limited range of options, and we aim at achieving one of those outcomes. A soccer match is an example of engagement through anticipation. The limited range of options are: (1) win or (2) lose. Most of the time, we want to win the game, so we do whatever we can to bring about—anticipate—that outcome. If you are a player on the team, you will yourself toward that outcome because no one has promised that you will win that game. This is anticipation in the absence of a promise. In this way, the future will be what you make of it, and your effort will determine what kind of future arrives. A majority of modern politics operates in the mode of anticipation. In the absence of a promised future, the future must be carved out by those willing to apply the most effort. There may be a future we want to have, and politics becomes our action in attempting to build it.

German philosopher Friedrich Nietzsche described this approach with exacting insight. Of course, Nietzsche is probably most well known for his adage "God is dead." What is often overlooked, however, is the way the rest of that sentiment progresses: "'Where is God? . . . I'll tell you! *We have killed him*—you and I!'"[2] The line is actually found in a philosophical parable, of sorts. The author imagines a John-the-Baptist-like figure standing in a town square, shouting to agreeable passersby who live their lives in relative comfort, making a way for themselves to be successful in the world. In their self-sufficiency, they have taken leave of their need for God. While they likely fill the pews of the local church buildings each week, their lives testify to their own achievements and a relative unwillingness to order their lives according to divine realities. They live as if they don't *need* God—therefore, they are the ones who have killed God.

Of course, this parable was used to describe real people who lived in Nietzsche's time. Nietzsche wasn't necessarily celebrating that "God was dead," as is often assumed, nor was he attempting to say that God had actually ceased to exist. Rather, he described how a generation was living, and the reality of what remained if we are going to live as though we do not need. Once we live like we don't need God, all we have left is our will. This, Nietzsche argued, would be the way things get done once we have decided to live as if we don't need God. One will is pitted against another, and the strongest of the two will ultimately be the one who gets to call the shots. Interestingly, Nietzsche then said that those who can amass enough power can will whatever they want—whatever they value.

2. Friedrich Nietzsche, *The Gay Science*, ed. Bernard Williams, trans. Josefine Nauckhoff (London: Cambridge University Press, 2003), 119–20.

I wonder how much of Nietzsche's vision has come to characterize the plight of Christian political engagement today. Have we unwittingly accepted Nietzsche's vision and become convinced that our political hope is found in amassing power so we can ultimately make a world that works for our interests? Do we feel as if we have to defeat others so we can succeed? Has a commitment to Jesus and his strange way been displaced by a quest to be the strongest voting bloc in the electorate?

The real issue for Christian ethics is that the Christian faith grows out of God's given *promise* of new creation that God has already opened to us in the resurrection of Jesus. This is the kind of future that doesn't need to be fought for according to the terms of the old creation. That promise sustained the first generation of those who followed the new creation that was opening in Jesus. Though they had their backs against a political wall—ignored, despised, or mocked by those in power—they continued to gather under the promise of a new political reality. For them, Jesus wasn't just someone who fit them into existing political realities. He offered them the politics of new creation. This was the politics that guided the early church's engagement in public life with a distinctive vision. As a group, these people were convinced that the resurrection of Jesus was real, that it had political implications for their time, and that they should bring that involvement to bear on the world around them. They stepped into the messy grit of public life, working their involvement toward new creation ends. Revelation, for example, oriented them to the promised reality. Letters like 2 Corinthians show how they were called to live that promise in their daily lives.

In Revelation, we see the new creation completed, and there's an unmistakably political shape. New creation comes as a city, arranged around a throne. A warrior king or ferocious lion do not occupy the throne, but a slaughtered

Lamb. His way is the way of new creation. The kings of the world lead their nations in joining the rhythms of life around the throne. Reconciliation marks the political life of new creation: humanity no longer works against God's purposes, and in being reconciled to God, they are reconciled to one another.

That promised politics is opened to the church even before the New Jerusalem is established. Writing to the little community of Christians gathering in Corinth a few years after the resurrection of Jesus, Paul attempts to help them see those realities. The book of 2 Corinthians is in part Paul's attempt to talk about the way money is handled in a post-resurrection world. The Christians meeting in Jerusalem are in need of money, and Paul is asking the Christians in Corinth to help. The tone of the letter is tense; Paul knows they are suspicious of him asking them to give him money to send to a group of people they've never met and who probably constitute a different racial identity. "Why should we give our money to *those* people?" you can almost hear them asking.

Paul helps them into the new world of moral possibility that the resurrection opens to them. "So from now on we regard no one from a worldly point of view," Paul tells them. "Though we once regarded Christ in this way, we do so no longer. Therefore, if anyone is in Christ, the new creation has come: The old has gone, the new is here!" (2 Cor. 5:16–17). For Paul, the resurrection has opened a reality in which these people who have never met and who occupy different racial realities are given the capacity to be reconciled to one another. That "ministry of reconciliation" (v. 18) isn't one that comes as a result of a really good conflict management system but is one that offers a new way of living, opened to us in the resurrection. This is, unmistakably, a new *political* reality that calls for the Corinthian Christians to arrange themselves in such a way as to be reconciled with their siblings in Jerusalem. This is more than altruism; it is action in accordance with the new creation that has been opened through the empty tomb.

As we work to discern politically with those around us, might we be able to do the work of political engagement with new creation in view? We can't build the New Jerusalem; it is a gift from God. Still, the completed city of the age to come offers us a political orientation. Can we work toward those realities in the midst of old creation? Are the political structures you support employed in the work of new creation God is bringing, or are they more attuned to someone's vision of simply trying to make old creation bend more easily toward their purposes? What if our politics weren't defined by who got our vote but by the way we engage in the new creation work of reconciliation across geographical, racial, economic, and national lines? What if we began to view politics itself not as being for winning a power struggle but for the purpose of new creation? What if our political engagement were not worked in *anticipation* of some outcome of our devising but as a grateful *reception* of the promise God has given in Christ's resurrection?

Questions for Discernment

1) How can we reimagine our political preferences if we find they do not aim at God's new creation?

2) How do your current political preferences guide you toward old creation (partisan loyalty) or new creation?

3) What if we imagine our community or church as a little *polis*? How would our politics in that situation reflect new creation?

4) Which course of action is most aligned with the way God is making the world new?

5) What practices can we put in place to live politically into new creation?

Resources for Further Exploration

Clapp, Rodney. *A Peculiar People: The Church as Culture in a Post-Christian Society*. Downers Grove, IL: InterVarsity Press, 1996).

Gaines, Timothy R. and Shawna Songer Gaines. *Kings and Presidents: Politics and the Kingdom of God*. Kansas City, MO: Beacon Hill Press of Kansas City, 2015.

Hendricks, Obery M. Jr., *The Politics of Jesus: Rediscovering the True Revolutionary Nature of the Teachings of Jesus and How They Have Been Corrupted*. New York: Doubleday, 2006.

Part II: Discerning the Work of Christian Ethics

Discernment Dialogue 5
Creation Care Ethics

Growing up among the agricultural fields of California's San Joaquin Valley, I lived between the pressures of the debates on environmental ethics. On one hand, there were groups who contended that the practices of modern agriculture were harmful to the earth. On the other side of the debate were those who didn't really disagree that the methods they were using had an impact on the environment but claimed that the needs of a booming population and their own livelihood as farmers outweighed the potential harm being done to the environment.

The unfortunate piece of this dynamic is that both sides tended to be locked in a fight for survival. In ethical terms, survival became the highest good for this fight. Christian ethics in the Wesleyan way doesn't make light of how precarious human survival can be, nor how serious an issue it is that our planet be able to sustain life. Mere survival, though, is not the highest good. Rather, Wesleyan ethics aims at the thriving of all creation, reminding humans that we are created in God's image and given a charge to care for creation. Additionally, creation is to be cared for not as a natural bank of finite resources but as the very arena in which God has chosen to relate to us.

Knowing we cannot do justice to such a complex topic in a short excursus, I want to propose a lens through which we can see the moral questions related to the care of cre-

The more excellent way challenges us to consider our consumption as an act of love.

ation. When we do the work of discernment, my hope is that we can rise above the back-and-forth power dynamic surrounding environmental ethics that is really just two sides of the same coin—a fight to survive.

Wesleyan theology tends to understand new creation to be the continuous work of God to make creation new, and it tends to see humans as agents and partners in that work. Rather than creation as the disposable background against which the human-centric drama of the world unfolds, creation is the very space that God hospitably opens so that something other than God can exist. God's love gratuitously opens a place for us to "live and move and have our being" (Acts 17:28), and in that place, we relate to God. If this world is the arena of relation that God has offered, the special role humans are given is to maintain it well so the love exchanged can flow freely. This reality extends not only to humans, but also to the rest of the created order. When creation is at its best, it allows for "all creatures of our God and King" to "lift up your voice and with us sing" praises to the God who has lovingly created well.[1] As part of that creation, humans do that work well when we are imaging God well. The "image of God" is a phrase borrowed from the creation narrative of Genesis 1, and is meant to evoke the image of a representative. As creatures *in God's image*, part of humanity's calling is to bear God's image to the rest of creation—to "re-present the covenantal character of the Creator, toward all of God's creatures."[2] In whatever way the rest of creation is capable of it, it can be reminded

---

1. Francis of Assisi, "All Creatures of Our God and King," trans. William H. Draper, *Sing to the Lord: Hymnal* (Kansas City, MO: Lillenas Publishing Company, 1993), #77.

2. Michael E. Lodahl and April Cordero Maskiewicz, *Renewal in Love: Living Holy Lives in God's Good Creation* (Kansas City, MO: Beacon Hill Press of Kansas City, 2014), 129.

of God's loving provision and the gift of life as it encounters that in humanity.

The fullest expression of this image was Jesus. "The Son is the image of the invisible God," we are told in Colossians, "the firstborn over all creation. For in him all things were created: things in heaven and on earth, visible and invisible, whether thrones or powers or rulers or authorities; all things have been created through him and for him" (1:15–16). Bearing the image and creation are inextricably linked in a biblically shaped imagination, and Jesus is the image of God *par excellence*. The enduring Wesleyan conviction that God's grace is capable of renewing us in God's image to make us more and more like Jesus has every implication for the way we relate to God's creation. Being renewed in God's image is to be a living reminder of the abundant life and plentitude of the garden. It is to join God's work of bringing creation to the point where the trees bear fruit in plenty and their leaves bring healing to the world (Rev. 22:2). It is to live a life so full of communion with God that God's purposes are worked out in our life together. To the ethical point, the more excellent way is to work toward the life-giving flourishing of creation and to care for it as an arena of God's blessing.

Hopefully we can see that this goes beyond arguments about what we ought to extract from the earth or leave in place in regard to survival, as important as survival is. A more excellent way is an ethics that goes beyond survival and toward thriving, extending an invitation to our neighbors into an arena where God and creation are related to one another in a dynamic of joy and flourishing. Additionally, this more excellent way is meant to challenge the temptation to think that there is no moral question when it comes to consuming whatever we can get our hands on. It challenges us to consider our consumption as an act of love. The problem is that modern moral philosophy rarely asks us to reflect like that. We are quietly formed to think that unchecked human consumption is as natural as a cat eating a mouse. As I heard a friend remark years ago, "If it's there and God made it, why can't we just take it?"

Three centuries ago, David Hume argued for a theory of moral sentiments, stating that humans can't be held to a higher moral account than what our nature allows. The natural feelings of compassion, for example, that are evoked when we see a beloved neighbor in need are natural to what it means to be human, and we ought to act on those sentiments. The fact that the same sentiments may not be evoked for someone we don't know or cannot see or do not like shouldn't be a moral problem. According to Hume, that's entirely natural. If we were to follow Hume on this point, the modern proclivity to hide society's most pernicious challenges to creation's well-being away from the gaze of everyday folks compounds a perplexing moral dilemma. For a majority of modern people living in developed countries, the effects of poverty and disease are hidden from view. Rather than suffering the effects of a painful disease at home among family and neighbors, we are often moved to hospitals, where friends and family have the option of visiting the sick, if they so choose. For those who earn steady incomes and live in middle-class housing, their daily routine rarely includes seeing how poverty, lack of access to groceries, or violence can erode communities only a few miles from their homes. If we don't *see* the way food is produced and harvested, we don't really have to think about it. If we can easily drive to a gas station but never see the way the processes required to extract the oil from the earth affect creation, we probably won't think twice. When the modern convenience of curbside trash pickup means we never have to see where the contents of the can are headed, it's doubtful our moral consciousness would ever be pricked.

It's not that modern people don't have sentiments—it's more that we rarely have the opportunity for those sentiments to be evoked. Few things could be more modern than the need to raise awareness of what our own actions are doing to the creation around us. The more excellent way calls for more than moral complacency. It calls us to be renewed in love and, in so doing, to be renewed in the image of God as caretakers of the arena.

Back to the farmlands of central California: I happen to be the grandson of Methodist farmers. The long country roads of Fresno County where they raised hogs, goats, and walnuts were made for big trucks. My grandparents drove a Prius. Every morning on the ranch began with a reading from Scripture before the day's work began. On a warm afternoon, I could walk through the shade of my grandfather's well-maintained walnut orchard, pass by the goose pens where we got our eggs, and then saunter through the robust vegetable garden that supplied their table. When I got to the house and went inside, I could find him in his chair at the end of the long day, reading a book about John Wesley. On the day of his memorial service, we gathered and remembered my grandfather as a man of uncommon patience. That's why we smiled when my own father rose to tell a story about a time his father-in-law's patience cracked. Toting a gun after some target practice, my dad saw a bird land nearby, raised the weapon, and fired.

The tone of my grandfather's voice was more frightening than the gunshot. "Hey! Don't you ever shoot a bird out here!"

Somewhere between the pages of Scripture, his Wesleyan heritage, and the vegetable garden, an *ethos* had taken hold of my grandfather. He was a man who worked the land and cared for birds. He drew from the earth and raised animals on it and wasn't interested in driving a car that wasn't fuel-efficient. It was as if he approached the world with a calling to tend it as a gardener, and in the garden, he himself became an image of the God who tends creation well. Perhaps this had plenty to do with the way he lived closely enough to see—really see—how his life was lived in relationship to the rest of creation. The slop bucket on the kitchen counter was where meal scraps went so the pigs wouldn't be hungry. If there was something that wasn't in their garden, my grandparents usually knew—by name— whose garden was growing it and how they could purchase it. It was probably also significant that, on the way to the fruit stand, they passed by a county landfill that took shape over the years of my childhood.

"That's Mount Trashmore," my grandmother would say as we passed by.

Actually seeing where their trash ended up wasn't lost on the ethos that shaped these two Wesleyans. They were people who were able to live an ethics—to do their work— in a way that wasn't merely about environmental ethics as a means of plundering the earth's resources or a desperate grasping at survival. There was something more. It was a vision, perhaps, of the goodness of God's creation, tended by faithful partners who knew in their theological bones that God had given them work to do—and so, work they did.

For a world that sits outside of and beyond the garden, distanced from the plentitude of its life-giving bounty of fruit and God's own presence, ever toiling to survive, a new creation people can be a means of grace-given life. A new creation people can image God to a groaning creation that has mistaken life for the fight to survive. Part of living as the image of God is to re-imagine environmental ethics as more than a strategy to survive but as the way abundant life is being offered to the whole world. Caring for creation is more than service to an environmental agenda of mere survival. Creation care is not a partisan power play that pits humans against one another in a ploy to preserve either the planet or our income. It is the work a people who have been formed and renewed in God's image can do to offer life-giving resource to our neighbors, and an arena of blessing where God and creation can dwell together. Especially in the likeness of Jesus, it is to image God, who opened graciously, giving others a place to thrive. At the end of that work, Wesley reminds us, is a new creation in which there is "a deep, an intimate, an uninterrupted union with God; a constant communion with the Father and his Son, Jesus Christ, through the Spirit; a continual enjoyment of the Three-One God, and of all the creatures in him!"[3]

Questions for Discernment

1) How can our community join the work of creation being made new in this situation?

2) When or how have we treated creation as a disposable reality rather than God's good gift? Which course of action allows others to enter into the arena of God's blessing more fully?

3) Where have we been lulled into blind consumption because we don't have to see its effects on others or the arena of creation? How can we open our eyes?

Resources for Further Exploration

Bouma-Prediger, Steven C. *For the Beauty of the Earth: A Christian Vision for Creation Care.* Grand Rapids: Baker Academic, 2010.

Lodahl, Michael E. and April Cordero Maskiewicz. *Renewal in Love: Living Holy Lives in God's Good Creation.* Kansas City, MO: Beacon Hill Press of Kansas City, 2014.

Richter, Sandra L. *Stewards of Eden: What Scripture Says about the Environment and Why It Matters.* Downers Grove, IL: InterVarsity Press, 2020.

---

3. Wesley, "The New Creation," *Works.*

Discernment Dialogue 6
Race, Culture, and Ethics

As I sit down to write this reflection, the headlines on cable news and my social media feeds are painfully punctuated with accounts of Ahmaud Arbery's death at the hands of some men who saw him jogging through their neighborhood, assumed he was a criminal, and pursued him with guns. Arbery—a black resident of Cobb County, Georgia—was shot and killed by a white man, the incident captured on video by another man who had joined the chase. Immediately, the story turned the spotlight on the way race shaped this incident. This was not the first time race would shape violent situations, and the agonizing reality we live in signals that Arbery's story would unfortunately not be the last.

I open with this story on an ethical excursus on race because it has likely awakened a response of some kind within you as you recall the situation. Heartbreak, frustration, confusion, and anger are all possible reactions. While there is no way that a short reflection in a book like this could possibly do any amount of justice to the way Christians have and might conceive of race in the formation of our ethics, I do want to at least offer a way to the work of discerning our ethics in light of race. I also offer it from what is unavoidably my own limited perspective as a white man who has been shielded from the pain and oppression so many of my friends have endured. While the meagerness of this offering will certainly not be up to the task of healing the pain racism has inflicted upon our world, I hope it will do something to call for doing the work of new creation.

Borrowing again from the primary approach I've used in this book, I want to suggest that the more excellent way offers a worthwhile challenge, especially to those who have not had to endure the pain of racialized oppression and violence. This is not meant to suggest an air of superiority, but it is to remind us that a Wesleyan way isn't satisfied with the bare minimum when it comes to the Christian life. Taken up in matters of race, "I'm not a racist" is not useful. The more excellent way is the refusal to excuse ourselves for meeting the bare minimum of not being overtly racist. The more excellent way is to allow the sanctifying grace of God to unearth, convict, and heal the precognitive reactions we have to those who are different from ourselves. It is to have the courage to not excuse ourselves but to borrow the words of the psalmist: "Search me, God, and know my heart; test me and know my anxious thoughts. See if there is any offensive way in me, and lead me in the way everlasting" (Psalm 139:23–24).

The precognitive reactions I have in mind are those that do not immediately dawn upon us in a conscious way. They are the feelings we get that make up the tapestry background of the way we interact with a person who carries a body that is different from our own. Robin Diangelo has likened this to becoming aware of a script that has been handed to us when we take the stage of life. "In this life," we could imagine it being said to two new actors, "you'll be playing the role of a black woman, and you'll be playing the role of a white man." As if on cue, we step into the expectations those roles carry in our fallen, old-creation world. Often, we don't know how to play anything *but* the role that has been handed to us. These, Diangelo notes, are "the unexamined beliefs that prop up our racial responses."[1] Perhaps even those who say with honesty that race had nothing to do with it still bear an unexamined set of beliefs that make up the background and move us into a script handed to us as we were born into a fallen, racialized world. These are the bone-deep assumptions that rarely surface but are always acting.

Alongside the math and reading (the cognitive) I learned as a child, I also learned to play the role that was handed to me when I was born into a racialized world. In the agricultural lands of central California, I learned to play the role of a white kid, juxtaposed with my classmates whose parents had emigrated from Mexico. While I took in lots of social lessons in the classroom about equality, there was a more complex reality being formed. Somewhere along the line, I silently came to expect that part of what it meant to be white was to be destined for college and a middle-class life of relative ease. What I wasn't aware of was that I was also forming a subtle and mostly silent expectation that my Mexican-American classmates were destined to do agricultural field work and live lives of hard labor. I came to expect that my European ancestral biology (Gaines is a very English name, and our skin tone matches it) somehow meant that I simply had a social role to fulfill. It wasn't the biological differences in my skin color from my classmates' that made me think this because, in all honesty, I wasn't *thinking* it at all. Rather, it was the way I became racialized in a precognitive sense.

Part of what I'm suggesting is that there isn't anything morally encoded in human DNA concerning race. I'm grateful for Brian Bantum's work, especially when he writes, "Race is not a history. Race is the story of our bodies, of our churches, of our faith. Race is a story that shapes the idea

---

1. Robin Diangelo, *White Fragility: Why It's So Hard for White People to Talk about Racism* (Boston: Beacon Press, 2018), 3.

of what our bodies are for."[2] Somewhere along the way, I learned that my body was for academic achievement and intellectual work and that the bodies of my Mexican-American friends were meant for something else. I didn't *think* that, but I *learned* it deeply. There's no way for me to know for sure, but I wonder if the men who reached for their guns when they saw Ahmaud Arbery jogging through their neighborhood became convinced he was a prowler because they were working the script that told them bodies with his kind of biological distinctions belonged to criminals.

This is why Robin Diangelo doesn't find much help in the lessons I was getting in school about merely respecting one another—the kind of lessons that teach us that the height of racial equality is to overlook or ignore our differences. "I don't see race," as I've heard it many times. That may be true, but that's precisely the problem. "Our simplistic definition of racism as intentional acts of racial discrimination committed by immoral individuals . . . engenders a confidence that we are not part of the problem and that our learning is thus complete."[3]

We shouldn't have to fear confessing this kind of script reception out loud. It's something old creation handed to us. Christian ethics in a Wesleyan mode can be shaped in the hope that new creation offers us a different role to play in a vastly different story. It's a mode of ethics that acknowledges that the old-creation racial script is often at odds with the new creation God is bringing, and it has enlisted us to play a role in its attempts to keep old creation old. The Wesleyan message is that God's grace has the capacity to turn agents of old creation—even unwitting ones—into agents of new creation.

---

2. Brian Bantum, *The Death of Race: Building a New Christianity in a Racial World* (Minneapolis: Fortress Press, 2016), 4–5.

3. Diangelo, *White Fragility*, 9.

Wesley was hopeful about the capacity of the means of grace to assist this work in us. Things like gathering with others to pursue a life of holiness and partaking of the Lord's Supper were activities charged with redemptive capacities. Early in the Wesleyan movement, those who gathered together to pursue a holy life saw that the racialized scripts handed to them kept them apart, even opposed to one another. Russell Richey has called some of these meetings between German and African Methodists "new creation business" that "did not respect the lines that the world drew, lines of language, class, and race."[4]

How might Christian communities engage in the work of ethics in a racialized world? At least one step may be to open ourselves to the reality that we have been recipients of old-creation scripts, complete with roles for us to play. When those are exposed as old-creation realities, a longing for a life of holiness should provide the courage for us to confess that we've been caught in those realities like a fly in a spider's invisible web, and we require the gentle rescue of a loving God who has the capacity to redeem us into agents of new creation. These agents will do the work of living a life that won't settle for old creation, even when old creation offers us the intoxicating anesthetic of privilege—the privilege of not having to pay the web much mind because the spider hasn't turned its sights on us yet. Another step would be to open ourselves to hear carefully, deeply, and unreservedly from those who have been forced to play a role in the script that was anything but reflective of the new creation. It may very well be that hearing well could be a means of grace, a call to confession and repentance, a call to reconciliation that is fu-

---

4. Russell E. Richey, "Methodism as New Creation" in M. Douglas Meeks, ed., *Wesleyan Perspectives on New Creation* (Nashville: Kingswood Books, 2004), 85.

eled with the holy courage to confess that we may have been playing a role in an unholy script.

A life of Christian holiness is a life that has come to know in a bones-deep way that the new creation opening to us in the way of Jesus may very well cost us the numbing repose of privilege scripted into the drama of old creation, but it will give us the only true life. The more excellent way is to move past "I'm not racist" and toward "Search me, God, and know my heart." In our discernment, Christians have no reason to fear taking account of the old-creation realities of race that put their hooks into us before we could speak. May God give us the words to confess how caught up we are, and the grace to turn those confessions into the reality of action.

Questions for Discernment

1) How or when have we unintentionally assigned moral purpose to certain biological characteristics of humans? How does that shape the way we interact with others?

2) When have we listened carefully and honestly to those who belong to a different race from ourselves about what their life is like? How can hearing from them allow the work of new creation to emerge in our community?

3) How can we open places for our brothers and sisters who belong to other races to speak honestly about what life is like for them? How can those in the racial majority hear them without becoming defensive or centering themselves in the conversation?

4) What kinds of power dynamics have emerged in our community around issues of race? Does our community (silently or otherwise) create a situation where racial minorities are not able to be a gift to our community in a full way?

5) How can we allow God to continue to work new creation in us, especially when it comes to the way we relate to those who are different from us?

Resources for Further Exploration

Bantum, Brian. *The Death of Race: Building a New Christianity in a Racial World*. Minneapolis: Fortress Press, 2016.

Diangelo, Robin. *White Fragility: Why It's So Hard for White People to Talk about Racism*. Boston: Beacon Press, 2018.

Jennings, Willie James. *The Christian Imagination: Theology and the Origins of Race*. New Haven, CT: Yale University Press, 2011.

Discernment Dialogue 7
Sexual and Family Ethics

While the ethical questions of sex, family, and marriage are too numerous and complex for us to deal with exhaustively here (see the book-length recommendations at the end of this chapter), some pressing general questions may help set

us down the path of discernment on these topics together:

What are marriage/family/sex *for*?

What is the purpose of family?

Do sexual relationships serve a purpose beyond themselves?

Where does singleness fit in this conversation?

Many approaches to an ethics of marriage, family, and sexuality have been proposed, though the Wesleyan tradition's emphasis on new creation may offer us a more excellent way to consider these questions. Taking this approach means that singleness, family, sex, and marriage can all be understood as a redemptive alignment of our lives to the world that God is making new. Each of these realities can serve as a living witness to what God is doing to make the world new. Each can be a holy glimpse of new creation, but first they will have to do more than serve themselves, or a vision of the good life that is disconnected from God's redemptive project. Aimed at some form of self-realization, family and sexual relationships have the capacity to turn in upon themselves in a feedback loop of dissatisfaction. Turned toward the purposes of God's new creation, however, they take on the capacity to be received and returned as a gift; they are given by God for the sake of loving neighbors.

Turning family, sex, and marriage toward new creation will first call for an alignment of the heart. Where the heart is aimed, the rest of our lives will follow. If our heart is aimed at marriage, sex, or family itself, our desire will terminate there, among the finite goods of the world. If, however, our heart is aimed at the infinite goodness of God, then family, marriage, and sex can be taken up as one aspect of a life that is turned toward a bottomless well of goodness and love. Singleness, marriage, and family could be means of walking the way of Jesus, rather than serving ourselves. While family, marriage, and sex can certainly be good, they are not the *ultimate* good and, as such, will never be able to deliver a life fully realized.

Throughout his life and in the midst of his own relational tribulations, John Wesley developed a notion that has a long history in the Christian tradition. In *A Plain Account of Christian Perfection*, Wesley wrote, "Here is the sum of the perfect law, the circumcision of the heart. Let the spirit return to God that gave it, with the whole train of affections."[1] The descriptive metaphor of a train evokes the image of something like a wedding dress, the train of which is pulled in the direction the wearer is walking. Wesley thought the human heart was similar. If the heart—the primary seat of motivation—is moving in the direction of God, all the other affections ought to follow after it.

Wesley's conflicted approach to romantic love demonstrated that he longed for a singleness of heart, devoted to God alone. Amidst the throes of romantic passion, he was concerned that his devotion to a woman would overtake

---

1. Wesley, *A Plain Account of Christian Perfection*, edited and annotated by Randy L. Maddox and Paul W. Chilcote (Kansas City, MO: Beacon Hill Press of Kansas City, 2015), 33.

his devotion to God, making what was primary second-ary. It wasn't simply that this was the right way to pursue relationship but that long tradition had taught Wesley that making a romantic relationship primary in his life would never be able to open a true life of goodness. The goods of romance, he knew, would become most potent when they became part of his devotion to God.

Long before Wesley, Augustine—another saint with a remarkably messy romantic history—reflected on his life and came to the conclusion that humans are wired for and propelled by desire. Desire, he said, wasn't a bad thing in and of itself. The question is what that desire is driving us toward. Ultimately, he said, the human heart will never be truly satisfied by anything we desire unless what we desire is the ultimate Good. That Good, for Augustine, was noth-ing other than God. "You have made us for yourself," he confessed to God, "and our heart is restless until it rests in you."[2] Search as we may, the human heart will never be at peace until it becomes primarily drawn toward the bound-less goodness that will never be exhausted. In the infinite goodness of the divine, human hearts can truly delight.

This means that all the finite things we may desire are not necessarily *bad* but that they will never bring true satisfaction to the human heart. Augustine's pastoral advice is to not mistake the ultimate Good for some other, second-ary good. Once we make that mistake, we are engaged in a fruitless attempt to find true satisfaction in something that is finite. As good as the dream job may be (or the house, or the car, etc.), it has its limits; it will never be able to offer the ever-expansive plentitude of joy and delight we find when we are "lost in wonder, love, and praise" of the di-

2. Augustine, *Confessions*, trans. Henry Chadwick (London: Oxford University Press, 2008), 3.

vine.[3] The same thing can be said of human relationships. While the modern message permeates popular culture that finding that special someone will somehow complete us, Pastor Augustine issues a sage warning: don't expect any human relationship to bring you the kind of ultimate joy and fulfillment the human heart longs for. This is not to say marriage, family, and sexuality are not good, but it is to say they are not the *ultimate* good.

How, then, should we conceive of the goods of marriage, sex, and family? Perhaps Wesley's own relational reticence can be helpful: let's be careful to not try to love anyone or anything other than God as if it is the ultimate good. Marriage, family, and sex, while goods, are not the *ultimate* good, and can be an aid to new creation as it finds its place in the train of affections being drawn primarily toward God. I say this against a background of popular Christian culture that has straddled a thin line between conceiving of marriage as *a* good while sometimes coming close to worshiping it as the *ultimate* good.

Early Christians, too, were working out what marriage was *for* in light of Christ's empty tomb and their cultural situation. With new creation in view, marriage didn't serve the survival of the Roman Empire or the personal preferences of individuals. Paul presents marriage and singleness as possible means of being disciples of the One who was making all things new. It is better for single men to remain single and for single women to remain single, Paul suggests in 1 Corinthians 7. Marriage, he says, is not a lesser or sinful state but, all things considered, he suggests remaining single if one can. "I am saying this for your own good," he writes, "not to restrict you, but that you may live in a right way in undivided devotion to the Lord" (v. 35). At the heart of Paul's moral instruction is the notion that devotion to

---

3. Charles Wesley, "Love Divine, All Loves Excelling," *Sing to the Lord*, #507.

the Lord is a higher good than marriage or sex. As he advises, marriage, sex, and singleness are meant to be avenues toward faithful devotion and discipleship. Should devotion to God be supported by singleness, then for Paul, that is the preferred option. The point is that family arrangements are not goods intended to serve themselves but are callings by which discipleship can be built up. When the heart is turned toward God, singleness, marriage, and sex will find their good place in the train of affections. The goodness of marriage and sex, are in whether they become an embodied witness to new creation. Should they detract from a life of faithfulness Paul recommends not pursuing them.

Jesus, too, understood the goods of marriage and family in terms of discipleship. "If anyone comes to me and does not hate father and mother, wife and children, brothers and sisters—yes, even their own life—such a person cannot be my disciple" (Luke 14:26). The word Luke uses here for "hate" (*miseo*) carries a morally comparative significance. It is a potent signal that loving a spousal or family relationship outside the dynamics of discipleship will short-circuit our ability to follow Jesus well.

German pastor and theologian Dietrich Bonhoeffer suggested the concept of mediation to help us grasp this reality. All of life's realities, he taught, are mediated to disciples *through* Jesus.[4] For the disciple, there are no *immediate* realities. We don't hold anything for ourselves, even our marital and family relationships. Christ is the center of life for disciples, holding all things together (Col. 1:17). When we think of family and sexual relationships, it is not simply that a husband is united to a wife or a child to a parent but that their relationship is mediated to each of them as they are held together in Christ. Our closest relationships come to us *through* and *in* Christ for the sake of something

4. See Dietrich Bonhoeffer, *Christ the Center* (New York: HarperOne, 2009).

Christian sexuality is fidelity as a witness to the faithfulness of Christ to the church. It is more about self-sacrifice than it is about self-realization.

beyond ourselves: the new creation. Therefore, marriage, family, and sex are not *for* us exclusively. Christian family commitments serve the purposes of new creation. Christian sexuality is a witness to the way all things are being made new in Christ. It is fidelity as a witness to the faithfulness of Christ to the church. It is more about self-sacrifice than it is about self-realization.

Advice like this can ring discordantly in the ears of modern people, probably because we have become accustomed to pursuing desires for family, marriage, and sex as goods for our own sake. We often consider marriage and sexuality in terms of what we gain, or in terms of our individual rights. Taking this approach turns the ethics of marriage and sex into what individuals should be allowed to do or pursue. The "culture wars" on marriage and sexuality have proceeded according to this logic, but we should remember that if the conversation is only about who should and shouldn't marry, we may miss the beautiful offering of the Christian faith: marriage is *for* new creation. It is a self-sacrificial offering to the rest of the world, giving our neighbors a living icon of God's covenantal faithfulness. Pastoral guidance to couples preparing for matrimony may need to include questions about whether they intend this union to be an offering poured out for the sake of blessing the world. Congregational discernment on family and marriage may need to include asking whether we are aiming toward new creation or for an image of the good life that we've inherited from society.

The pastoral wisdom of Wesley and Augustine calls to us: even if you get the family arrangement you want, it won't ultimately satisfy you! Knowing the goodness and joy of singleness, marriage, or sex calls for us to pursue them as avenues of God's infinite goodness, rather than for what we might get out of them. If we locate them in the train of affections that is singularly aimed toward the goodness of

God, they can be employed as means of grace, discipleship, and the ability to reflect well the image of God. Marriage can be a living icon of God's covenantal faithfulness to creation. Singleness can be an image of full devotion to the work of New Creation. Family can be offered as a long life of hospitality to children and the aged. Sex can be self-giving, rather than self-serving, especially when it is a means of welcoming children. Additionally, this means marriage and singleness can equally serve the virtuous ends of discipleship. To appeal to Paul's instruction, sex, marriage, and family are *for* discipleship. If one needs to remain single for this to happen, singleness can be considered a good on its way to a greater good. Marriage, too, finds its true north as it directs both partners into a fuller estate of devotion to God.

The attempt to take any of these secondary goods— marriage, family, sex—as if they are going to provide ultimate fulfillment will be a frustrating, fruitless, even idolatrous enterprise. Still, generations of Christians have received implicit and explicit messages that human fulfillment lies in achieving the right arrangement of our sexual lives. The picture of the American dream has taken hold of our moral imaginations and repeated an enduring message: *Fulfillment will come when you find that special someone, get married, and have kids. That's the good life.* The vision of the good life in Christian ethics is faithfully walking the way where Jesus is making things new. Augustine reminds us that our restless hearts will not find rest in marriage, family, or sex until those hearts are fully devoted to God. Additionally, making the institution of marriage or parenthood the object of the fulfilled life will perpetually deny fulfillment to those who cannot or will not marry, those who are incapable of having children, or those whose sexual desires do not fit such an image. If we were to take a page from Wesley (who was guided on this by Augustine), we would find that happiness—true, joyful happiness—is holiness. It is the estate of enduring devotion to God, a heart fully turned toward the divine. This means that marriage and singleness share an equal capacity to be a holy estate. They are both welcome in the train of affections.

While marriage is called to be a holy estate, its holiness is in its service to God's purposes. Jesus indeed blessed a wedding in Cana with his presence, but he also called marriage to serve something beyond the desires of the husband and wife for one another. The wine that flowed from the jars that day was a sign of life, an overflow of blessing poured out upon those around the couple. When Jesus blesses a marriage, he transforms it into a feast of grace—something that's meant to be poured out for the sake of others—and, in so doing, reveals his glory through the marriage (see John 2).

The holiness of marriage is found in the way it serves something beyond itself: devotion to God's new creation. Its holiness is in the way it reflects and joins the pattern of Jesus, who gave himself for the church while making the world new. The faithfulness of marriage serves as an embodied and enduring witness to Christ's self-giving and sacrificial love. Christian marriage is a vocation—a calling to give your life in mutual love and submission as a window into the self-giving love of God. When our family and sexual arrangements serve this kind of vocational purpose, singleness can be every bit as holy as marriage. Paul's preferred option was just that precisely because he understood it to be more readily equipped for devotion to Christ. If devotion to God is the primary longing of our heart, then perhaps we could discover that singleness is neither morally superior nor inferior to marriage. Perhaps we could see that marriage and family can be understood as *vocations* to which we are called for the sake of discipleship.

The questions that might guide our moral discernment regarding these issues ask what singleness, marriage, sex, and family are *for*. Singleness can be a gift serving full devotion to God. Marriage can be a calling to show forth in our own bodies what it looks like to give away your own desires for the sake of another. Parenthood can be more about offering hospitality to little disciples than fulfilling our desire to "*have* kids." Dedicating and baptizing our children reminds us that they are never ours to possess but that parents are called to move our children to a life of discipleship. They belong to God, and we are helping them along the way.

Sexual practice, too, turns in upon itself when it is pursued for its own sake. If it reduces to self-gratification, it closes off the possibility of being a window to the life of the divine, a train of affections simply going in circles without ever arriving at delight. If sexual practice flows out of a heart devoted to God, a world of possibility dawns on our moral imagination. Among the contemporary moral debates regarding sexual and family rights, perhaps the church can also open a line of moral inquiry into what sex, family, and marriage are *for* in the first place. That will call upon us to release whatever remaining impulse we have to turn marriage into an idol, parenthood into our ultimate purpose, or to treat sex like it is life's goal. But it may also allow us to turn our hearts to the Lord and let our practices of sex, marriage, and family be the embodied steps of our devotion.

Questions for Discernment

1) What are sex, marriage, or family *for*? What might change if we saw their purpose as part of being a disciple of Jesus?

2) How might we encourage those involved to consider this issue a matter of discipleship?

3) How have we unwittingly treated marriage, sex, and family as ends in themselves?

4) How have we created or contributed to a culture where marriage is seen as better than singleness? When have we participated in the narrative that singleness is better than marriage?

5) What might happen if we began to discern marriage, singleness, and parenthood as vocations to which we are called for the sake of discipleship? How might we consider them if they were certain forms of imaging God to the world?

Resources for Further Exploration

Coakley, Sarah. *God, Sexuality, and the Self: An Essay 'On The Trinity.'* Cambridge: Cambridge University Press, 2013.

Jones, Beth Felker. *Faithful: A Theology of Sex.* Grand Rapids: Zondervan, 2015.

Paris, Jenell Williams. *The End of Sexual Identity: Why Sex Is Too Important to Define Who We Are.* Downers Grove, IL: IVP Books, 2011.

Wong, Bernard K. *Beginning from Man and Woman: Witnessing Christ's Love in the Family.* Carlisle, United Kingdom: Langham Monographs, 2017.

Bibliography

Aristotle, *Aristotle's Nichomachean Ethics*, Robert C. Bartlett & Susan D. Collins, eds. Chicago: University of Chicago Press, 2012.

Augustine, *Confessions*, trans. Henry Chadwick. London: Oxford University Press, 2008.

Bantum, Brian. *The Death of Race: Building a New Christianity in a Racial World*. Minneapolis: Fortress Press, 2016.

Beck, Richard. *Unclean: Meditations on Purity, Hospitality, and Morality*. Eugene, OR: Cascade Books, 2011.

Bewkes, Eugene Garrett and James Calvin Keene. *The Western Heritage of Faith and Reason*. New York: Harper & Row, 1963.

Bondi, Roberta. "Praying the Lord's Prayer: Truthfulness, Intercessory Prayer, and Formation in Love." *Liturgy and the Moral Self: Humanity at Full Stretch before God*, Bruce T. Morrill and E. Byron Anderson, eds. Collegeville, MN: Liturgical Press, 1998.

Bonhoeffer, Dietrich. *Christ the Center*. New York: HarperOne, 2009.

Borgmann, Albert. *Power Failure: Christianity in the Culture of Technology*. Grand Rapids: Brazos Press, 2003.

Bouma-Prediger, Stephen C. *For the Beauty of the Earth: A Christian Vision for Creation Care*. Grand Rapids: Baker Academic, 2010.

Boyd, Craig and Don Thorsen. *Christian Ethics and Moral Philosophy: An Introduction to Issues and Approaches*. Grand Rapids: Baker Academic, 2018.

Clapp, Rodney. *A Peculiar People: The Church as Culture in a Post-Christian Society*. Downers Grove, IL: InterVarsity Press, 1996.

Clapper, Gregory Scott. *John Wesley on Religious Affections: His Views on Experience and Emotion and Their Role in the Christian Life and Theology*. Metuchen, NJ: Scarecrow Press, 1989.

Coakley, Sarah. *God, Sexuality, and the Self: An Essay 'On The Trinity.'* London: Cambridge University Press, 2013.

Collins, Kenneth J. *A Faithful Witness: John Wesley's Homiletical Theology*. Wilmore, KY: Wesley Heritage Press, 1993.

Deschner, John. *Wesley's Christology*. Wilmore, KY: Francis Asbury Press, 1985.

Diangelo, Robin. *White Fragility: Why It's So Hard for White People to Talk about Racism*. Boston: Beacon Press, 2018.

Dunning, H. Ray. *Reflecting the Divine Image: Christian Ethics in Wesleyan Perspective*. Eugene, OR: Wipf and Stock, 2003.

Fee, Gordon and Douglas Stuart. *How to Read the Bible for All Its Worth*. Grand Rapids: Zondervan Academic, 2014.

Fretheim, Terrence. *New Interpreter's Bible*. Nashville: Abingdon Press, 1994.

Gaines, Timothy R. and Shawna Songer Gaines. *Kings and Presidents: Politics and the Kingdom of God*. Kansas City, MO: Beacon Hill Press of Kansas City, 2015.

Hauerwas, Stanley. *God, Medicine, and Suffering*. Grand Rapids: William B. Eerdmans Publishing Company, 1990.

Hauerwas, Stanley and Samuel Wells, eds. *The Blackwell Companion to Christian Ethics*. Oxford: Blackwell Publishing, 2006.

Hays, Richard. *The Moral Vision of the New Testament: A Contemporary Introduction to New Testament Ethics*. San Francisco: HarperSanFrancisco, 1996.

Hendricks, Obery M. Jr. *The Politics of Jesus: Rediscovering the True Revolutionary Nature of the Teachings of Jesus and How They Have Been Corrupted*. New York: Doubleday, 2006.

Hume, David. *A Treatise of Human Nature*, David Norton, ed. London: Oxford University Press, 2011.

Jennings, Theodore W. Jr. *Good News to the Poor: John Wesley's Evangelical Economics*. Nashville: Abingdon Press, 1990.

Jennings, Willie James. *The Christian Imagination: Theology and the Origins of Race*. New Haven, CT: Yale University Press, 2011.

Jenson, Robert. *A Theology in Outline: Can These Bones Live?* New York: Oxford University Press, 2016.

Jones, Beth Felker. *Faithful: A Theology of Sex*. Grand Rapids: Zondervan, 2015.

_____. *Practicing Christian Doctrine: An Introduction to Thinking and Living Theologically*. Grand Rapids: Baker Academic, 2014.

Lodahl, Michael E. *God of Nature and of Grace: Reading the World in a Wesleyan Way*. Nashville: Abingdon Press, 2003.

Lodahl, Michael E. and April Cordero Maskiewicz. *Renewal in Love: Living Holy Lives in God's Good Creation.* Kansas City, MO: Beacon Hill Press of Kansas City, 2014.

Lovin, Robin. *Christian Ethics: An Essential Guide.* Nashville: Abingdon Press, 2000.

MacIntyre, Alasdair. *Whose Justice? Which Rationality?* Notre Dame, IN: University of Notre Dame Press, 1988.

Maddox, Randy L. *Responsible Grace: John Wesley's Practical Theology.* Nashville: Kingswood Books, 1994.

Marquardt, Manfred. *John Wesley's Social Ethics: Praxis and Principles,* trans. John E. Steely & W. Stephen Gunter. Nashville: Abingdon Press, 1992.

Meilander, Gilbert. *Bioethics: A Primer for Christians.* Grand Rapids: William B. Eerdmans Publishing Company, 2004.

Míguez, Néstor. "The Old Creation in the New, the New Creation in the Old." *Wesleyan Perspectives on the New Creation,* M. Douglas Meeks, ed. Nashville: Kingswood Books, 2004.

Nietzsche. Friedrich. *The Gay Science,* Bernard Williams, ed. London: Cambridge University Press, 2003.

Oden, Thomas. *John Wesley's Teachings: Ethics and Society.* Grand Rapids: Zondervan, 2014.

O'Donovan, Oliver. *Finding and Seeking: Ethics as Theology.* Grand Rapids: William B. Eerdmans Publishing Company, 2014.

_____. *The Ways of Judgment.* Grand Rapids: William B. Eerdmans Publishing Company, 2008.

Ott, Kate. *Christian Ethics For a Digital Society.* Lanham, MD: Rowman & Littlefield, 2019.

Otto, Rudolph. *The Idea of the Holy,* trans. John W. Harvey. London: Oxford University Press, 1923.

Paris, Jenell Williams. *The End of Sexual Identity: Why Sex Is Too Important to Define Who We Are.* Downers Grove, IL: IVP Books, 2011.

Plato. *Five Dialogues: Euthyphro, Apology, Crito, Meno, Phaedo,* trans. G. M. A. Grube, rev. John M. Cooper, 2nd ed. Indianapolis: Hackett Publishing Company, Inc., 2002.

Richey, Russell E. "Methodism as New Creation." *Wesleyan Perspectives on New Creation,* M. Douglas Meeks, ed. Nashville: Kingswood Books, 2004.

Richter, Sandra. *Stewards of Eden: What Scripture Says about the Environment and Why It Matters.* Downers Grove, IL: IVP Academic, 2020.

Runyon, Theodore. *Exploring the Range of Theology*. Eugene, OR: Wipf and Stock, 2012.

_____. "The New Creation: A Wesleyan Distinctive." *Wesleyan Theological Journal*. Vol. 31 No. 2. Fall 1996.

Saliers, Don. "Liturgy and Ethics: Some New Beginnings." *Journal of Religious Ethics*. Vol. 7 No. 2. Fall 1979.

Smith, Adam. *The Wealth of Nations*. New York: Bantam Classics, 2003.

Tanner, Kathryn. *Christianity and the New Spirit of Capitalism*. New Haven, CT: Yale University Press, 2019.

Tertullian. "On Prescriptions against Heretics." *Ante-Nicene Fathers*, Alexander Roberts and James Donaldson, eds. Peabody, MA: Hendrickson Publishers, 2004.

Verhey, Allen. *Remembering Jesus: Christian Community, Scripture, and the Moral Life*. Grand Rapids: William B. Eerdmans Publishing Company, 2002.

Waters, Brent. *Just Capitalism: A Christian Ethic of Economic Globalization*. Louisville: Westminster John Knox Press, 2016.

_____. *This Mortal Flesh: Incarnation and Bioethics*. Grand Rapids: Brazos Press, 2009.

Watson, Kevin and Scott Kisker. *The Band Meeting: Rediscovering Relational Discipleship in Transformational Community*. Franklin, TN: Seedbed Publishing, 2017.

Wesley, John. "Of Preaching Christ." *John Wesley*, Albert C. Outler, ed. London: Oxford University Press, 1980.

_____. *The Works of John Wesley*. Thomas Jackson, 3rd edition. Grand Rapids: Baker Books, 2005.

Willimon, William H. and Stanley Hauerwas. *Lord, Teach Us: The Lord's Prayer and the Christian Life*. Nashville: Abingdon Press, 2010.

Wong, Bernard K. *Beginning from Man and Woman: Witnessing Christ's Love in the Family*. Carlisle, United Kingdom: Langham Monographs, 2017.

Wynkoop, Mildred Bangs. *A Theology of Love*, 2nd edition. Kansas City, MO: Beacon Hill Press of Kansas City, 2015.

www.ingramcontent.com/pod-product-compliance
Lightning Source LLC
Chambersburg PA
CBHW070037100426
42740CB00013B/2717